MICHAEL EATON

LIVING UNDER GRACE

PREACHING THROUGH ROMANS

ROMANS 6:1-7:25

LIVING UNDER GRACE

PREACHING THROUGH ROMANS

ROMANS 6:1-7:25

WORD PUBLISHING
Nelson Word Ltd.
Milton Keynes, England
WORD AUSTRALIA
Kilsyth, Australia
NELSON WORD CANADA
Vancouver, B.C., Canada
STRUIK CHRISTIAN BOOKS (PTY) LTD.
Cape Town, South Africa
JOINT DISTRIBUTORS SINGAPORE-
ALBY COMMERCIAL ENTERPRISES PTE LTD.
and
CAMPUS CRUSADE, ASIA LTD.
PHILIPPINE CAMPUS CRUSADE FOR CHRIST
Quezon City, Philippines
CHRISTIAN MARKETING NEW ZEALAND LTD.
Havelock North, New Zealand
JENSCO LTD.
Hong Kong
SALVATION BOOK CENTRE
Malaysia

LIVING UNDER GRACE

Published in the UK by Nelson Word Ltd., Milton Keynes, England, 1994.

ISBN 0-85009-703-7

Reproduced, printed and bound in Great Britain for Nelson Word Ltd. by Cox & Wyman Ltd., Reading.

94 95 96 97 / 10 9 8 7 6 5 4 3 2 1

CONTENTS

PREFACE

These expositions of Romans chapters 6 and 7 are abridged versions of 'messages' originally preached during 1993. I would like to think that they will help preachers, because they were preached. I generally speak for about an hour; these studies represent the main points only. They are part of a project that I have to publish my third exposition of Romans. The first time I preached through Romans was in the adult Bible class of Lusaka Baptist Church, over the course of four years. Then some years later I took just over a year to give weekly expositions on Romans, which went out over Trans-World Radio from Swaziland. At about the same time worshippers at Nairobi Baptist Church heard fifteen sermons on Romans 12. Then in 1988 I started on Romans again, in various fellowships in Nairobi, mainly the Nairobi City Hall meetings of the Chrisco Fellowship of Churches, and I have been preaching on-and-off through Romans ever since. It is this version which is reproduced here, in slightly modified form. Spin-offs and condensed versions have been heard in Stoneleigh Bible Week, and in the New Frontiers Training Centre in Goa, India.

My more recent expositions are less legalistic, have a clearer approach (I hope!) to Romans 7, a totally different approach to Romans 2:14–16, a clearer exposition of Romans 13:8–10. I have moved position over some issues. There is one thing worse than a preacher who changes his mind and that is a preacher who never changes his mind!

Numerous articles and works on Paul have helped me, and I have had twenty-four commentaries on Romans within reach, as well as those consulted in libraries, plus my own previous expositions which I have reconsidered along the way. Scholarly readers may like to know that the works on 'The New Perspective on Paul' by Sanders, Dunn and others have been pondered. I think they are right in affirming that the cultural aspect of Paul's teaching needs considering, but I still think the Reformation approach to Paul is fruitful and basically correct. I appreciate that the 'New Perspective' has opened up some important matters of interpretation.

In connection with the sixth chapter of Romans I must mention the brilliant expositions in Dr D. M. Lloyd-Jones' book *The New Man* (Banner of Truth, 1972). His approach to 'baptism' in Romans 6:3 is controversial, but I am sure it is right. It is encouraging that Dr James Dunn takes a similar view (in the *Word Biblical Commentary, Romans 1—8*, pp.303, 311–313 as well as in previous works referred to there).   John Brown's commentary of 1857 took the same approach.   However I do not follow Dr Lloyd-Jones slavishly; I have rather tried to build on his exegesis and press on to greater accuracy.   While preaching on this section I worked through Thomas Manton's sermons on Romans 6 preached more than 300 years ago.   Modern study is more accurate, yet Manton is my favourite Puritan and I have had volume 11 of his works at hand during the preparation of this material.

Dr Lloyd-Jones' book *The Law: Its Functions and Limits* (Banner of Truth, 1973) was at my finger tips during the preaching of this material, although my measure of agreement with it is less.   His interpretation is stimulating, but leaves difficult questions.   He repeatedly says the 'wretched man' of 7:14–25 is neither regenerate or unregenerate.   This is not a slip of the tongue.   He puts it most strongly.   'I assert that it is neither the unregenerate nor the regenerate' (p. 192).   Dr Lloyd-Jones held that the Spirit could take time in bringing a person to faith. It was this that led him to use such phrases as 'neither regenerate or unregenerate' or not 'completely regenerate'.   I disagree with this.   For me, verse 5 makes it clear.   The person concerned is 'in the flesh', and unregenerate.   Dr Lloyd-Jones' line of thought would have been clearer, I believe, if he had said that the person concerned is unregenerate but is not the normal unregenerate person but one of the few seeking to be holy by the law.

I also disagree with Dr Lloyd-Jones in another matter. Although he disliked Roman Catholicism, he held to Thomas Aquinas's view of 'the moral law' (see chapter 30) and regarded a 'Romans 7' experience as compulsory (although he did not wish to demand any particular measure of intensity of the experience).   And he held the Reformed view that you have to come under the law before you are truly saved.   I do not agree with this approach and think it is introspective.   However he went much further than his Reformed colleagues in saying clearly that 'sanctification by the Law is as impossible as was justification by the law' (p. 4), and his remark that Romans 7:7–13 is an elaboration of verse 5 (p. 171) I regard as exactly right.   I feel I am walking further in the direction to which he pointed. Certainly those who know Dr Lloyd-Jones' writings will recognise their influence and realise that my expositions are a kind of running debate, sometimes in agreement, sometimes going my own way. Young Christians will certainly be confused by Dr Lloyd-Jones' *The Law,* but expositors will learn some things from it. My conclusion is: his grasp of exegetical detail in this chapter is marvellous but his final overall doctrine of the law is unsatisfactory and too introspective. I have tried to improve on his exposition—but have been standing on his shoulders. I was glad I had the support of R.C.H.Lenski's *Romans* in translating verse 14 'I know' rather than 'We know'.

In the second half of this work I have tried to deal with controversies concerned with 'the law' in as simple manner as I can but realise that some chapters still require more than one reading before they will be grasped. Chapters 30, 35, 44 and 45 are more technical than usual and can be skipped at a first reading.

Although scholarly writings are my daily food, there is no scholarly apparatus in this book. It tries to be free from distractions. All translations from the Bible are my own. On the other hand I know well the various revisions of the Authorised Version. If my translations resemble that tradition I shall not be surprised.

My wife has encouraged my many years of Romans study. I continue to be grateful for her helping forward this project, and I generally accept the suggestions she makes as I write. She puts up with my strange habits of tapping away on a computer sometimes in the middle of the night, and supplies (at more reasonable hours) cups of Kenya chai to keep me going. My son, Calvin Eaton, has given his time and his expertise with computers to this project, and has rescued me from various word-processing crises. What would I do without him? I am especially grateful to friends who have read parts of the manuscript, and commented on it for me, checking for simplicity, making suggestions and generally keeping me motivated and encouraged as I have been preaching through Romans. This work is the better for their recommendations as I write and preach. They are precious to me indeed. Mrs Florence Okumu, with her eagle's eyes, has worked through the whole for me; I am grateful.

As for the Chrisco people of Nairobi for whom this material was preached and written—Heaven will reveal how much I love you but I am doing my best to reveal it now!

Michael Eaton, Nairobi, May 1994

PART ONE

Romans 6:1–23b

HOW IMPORTANT IS GODLINESS?
(Romans 6:1–2a)

How important is it to live a godly life? This is the question that arises in our minds if we are reading the first five chapters of the letter to the Romans with understanding. Paul himself raises it, because he knows we shall be thinking of it. He says: What shall we say, therefore?—in the light of what we have seen so far—Are we to continue in sin, in order that grace may abound? (Rom. 6:1) Why should Paul have to ask this question? Is there anyone who thinks we should continue in sin? Paul's answer is sharp: Let it not be! (Rom. 6:2a).

The reason for the question is what Paul has said so far in his letter. The gospel often seems to be casual about righteousness and holiness. Actually, Jesus came 'in order to redeem us from all lawlessness and in order that He might purify for himself a people of his own possession who are zealous about good works' (Titus 2:14). The last chapters of this great letter (12:1 to 15:13) are a sustained call to live out the godly life in many different areas. We are to be yielded to God (12:1–2), to serve the Lord in the fellowship (12:3–8) and in a whole range of varying situations (12:9–21). We are to obey the 'powers that be', the civic authorities (13:1–7), and are to fulfill the Mosaic law by living the life of love (13:8–10), and so on.

Yet salvation is 'without works'. We are not brought into our initial salvation by godliness. We are kept safe in salvation by Jesus, not by how godly we are. 'Justification' is without works. We are given a gift of righteousness. The very moment we believe, we are covered over before God, with the righteousness of Jesus. When we believe in Jesus the Son of God, it is immediately as though we had never sinned, as though we were as righteous as Jesus. Paul does not mention good works or sanctification or repentance (Rom. 1:17).

There is a righteousness that comes from God, he said in

chapter 3:21, that is without keeping any of the moral principles of the law given through Moses, and without the religious ceremonies of the tabernacle. He said we could be 'justified'— declared righteous—'freely, as a gift' (Rom. 3:24). We are not saved by our turning from sin; we are saved by the righteousness and blood of Jesus. Our repentance is not perfect, but the righteousness of Jesus is perfect.

I remember some years ago having to interview a lot of people concerning their salvation. I would ask them, 'Tell me how you were saved and became a Christian.' Often people would say to me, 'Well, I used to live a wicked life and then I repented and I got saved.' In that testimony Jesus is not even mentioned! It seems as though that person saved himself! But we are not our own saviours; Jesus is the Saviour. Our testimony—if we are Christians—is that we were nothing and could do nothing to save ourselves but then God showed us Jesus and we put our trust in Him and now we stand righteous before God because we are clothed in the righteousness of Jesus. Our sins are forgiven because of the cleansing blood of Jesus. Jesus! Jesus! He is the Saviour, not we ourselves or our good works—'Being justified freely through the redemption that is in Christ Jesus'. In 3:28 we have it again: 'a person is justified by faith apart from the works of the law'. Abraham believed God and that was reckoned to him for righteousness (4:3). Imagine you have a job. You are working hard for an employer. By the end of a month you have worked well. Now you are eager to collect your wages. But the employer seems very casual. 'Well I'm not planning to give you anything. But I'll give you a gift to keep you going.' What would you say? 'What do you mean, you'll give me a gift?' you say to him. 'I don't want a gift. I want my wages, my salary. I have worked hard for it. You owe it to me.' That is Paul's argument. 'When a person works his wages are not credited to him as a gift' (Rom. 4:4). But the point is that salvation does not come by a person's working. It comes freely. It is not earned; it is a gift. To the person who does nothing but believes, his faith is reckoned as righteousness. That is the way of salvation! We are credited with righteousness without works (4:6).

In Romans chapter 5 Paul goes further. We have peace with God and a certainty of getting to glory. We have been saved from God's wrath. We are reconciled. We shall be saved by Jesus' life. We are in Christ, and the grace of God is so much stronger and greater than the sin that ruled us when we were in Adam. In chapter 5:16 he actually said that the gift of being right with God comes 'following many trespasses'. We may have sinned thousands of times, but when we were joined to Jesus salvation came to us 'following many trespasses'. No matter how much we sinned God's grace can overrule. The law of God came in to increase the trespass but 'where sin abounded grace abounded all the more' (5:20). What an amazing description of the grace of God! No matter how much we have sinned the amazing grace of God is there to restore and to keep. Now we can surely understand Paul's question. However far we go in sin the grace of God is bigger. Does this mean that God's grace will go on and on and abound so much, we may as well not bother about resisting sin at all! Perhaps it will make no difference whether we sin or not? Paul's answer is sharp: Let it not be! We must live a godly life. The grace of God is there to get us out of sin not to encourage us in it. The grace of God is there to save you, forgive you, cleanse you, pick you up and then get you out of your sins altogether.

A MISUNDERSTOOD GOSPEL
(Romans 6:1–2a)

I wonder, is your sharing or preaching the gospel ever misunderstood? Is it ever thought to be carelessness about sin?

Of course, no one wants their way of putting the gospel to be misunderstood, but Paul's doctrine of grace was so 'extreme' that it gave rise to the question *Are we to continue in sin, in order that grace may abound?* (Rom. 6:1). Paul's answer is No! Not at all! *Let it not be!* (Rom. 6:2a). But there is always someone who says, 'You are preaching that we can do what we like and get away with it.' When you preach the gospel properly you are likely to be misunderstood. Someone is likely to say, 'You are preaching grace too much. You are preaching that we can just sin.' I hope you are *not* saying that, but the true gospel of God's amazing grace is liable to misunderstanding. They misunderstood Paul, they misunderstood Jesus. Do they misunderstand you? If they don't have any problem with you, are you preaching the gospel of Jesus? If you are preaching what Jesus and Paul preached you will get misunderstood in the same way. My question is: do you have such a high doctrine of the wonderful, amazing, overwhelming grace of God that people (falsely) jump to the conclusion that you are tolerating sin? People do not easily understand that grace trains us to live godly lives. They think that talk about grace means that we can sin as much as we like. Those of us who love to preach on the gospel of God's grace are *not* preaching that grace encourages sin. Yet the grace of God is so wonderful that you must not be surprised if people misunderstand. There will always be someone who will say, 'Ah, but you are justifying sin!' I am not trying to answer the point at the moment. Paul will go on to do that in the rest of Romans chapter 6.

Jesus had the same problem. 'Don't think', He said, 'that I have come to destroy the law. I have come to fulfil it by giving you my resurrection power. I, Jesus, not the law of Moses, am telling you what you should do. I will be with you to the end of the age. You are under my leading, my instruction. You are not under the law but I am not *destroying* the law.' Why did anyone think that perhaps Jesus had come to destroy the law? It was because He preached such a message of free salvation. There was such grace in His preaching. He could say to the woman caught in adultery, 'I don't condemn you. Go and sin no more.' But the Pharisees felt that Jesus' message was too easy. 'This is easy-believism,' they said. (Did they think the gospel was 'difficult-believism'?)

The one and only gospel is so full of God's amazing grace that it can be misunderstood along these lines. Romans chapter 6 is Paul's reply. First, he gives a basic answer. We have died to sin; it is not logical or in accord with what God has done to us for us to go on in sin (Rom. 6:2). Then he works out what this means in fuller detail. We have been placed into Christ. We are joined on to His death and His resurrection and to everything about Him. Jesus cannot fall into the realm of sin. We are in Him and so we have died to sin in Him and we are alive to God in Him (Rom. 6:3–10). Paul asks us to reckon upon this being true and therefore to co-operate with God and not yield to sin's demands (6:11–14).

Then Paul comes back at the question a second time. Can we go on in sin? No! (6:15). But now he deals with the matter more practically. He argues with us that we should yield ourselves to God. Yielding leads to bondage of one kind or another (6:16), whether the horrible bondage of sin, or the sweetness of being Jesus' 'slave'. This is true even if we have died to sin! The basic change of position has been made (6:17–18). He appeals to us to actually yield ourselves to God (6:19). He asks us to think of the outcome of the old life (6:20–21) and of the new life (6:22) and ends the chapter by contrasting what the old life brought and what the new life will bring (6:23). The gist of the whole is clear. Can we go on in sin? No! We are under the rule of God's grace. God's grace abounds more than most of us have ever dreamed of. But does this mean that we can continue in sin? No. It is not *impossible* to sin, but it is foolish, illogical, rebellious. And it has consequences that will last for ever. God wants to minister to us the blessings of eternal life. Paul will give us reasons why we shouldn't, why we mustn't go on in sin, why we must let the abounding grace of God lead us gently, sweetly, without forcing our wills, into a life of sanctification, godliness, fruitfulness. God wants to go on giving us His free, eternal life, and that includes a life of godliness. There is something that makes a casual approach to sin quite impossible. We have died to sin. We have been transferred to a new realm where God's grace rules over us. The only logical thing to do is to work that out in a life of practical, godly living.

WE DIED TO SIN
(Romans 6:2b)

For a Christian to go on in sin is inconsistent with what has happened to him. Admittedly, it is not *impossible*. The New Testament has many examples of sinning Christians. Every letter of the New Testament shows us the possibility of the Christian's falling into even serious sin. But the Christian has 'died to sin'. When we are under the grace of God, we are in a *position* where it is possible to resist sin. Grace does not encourage us to go on in sin. Far from it! Paul tells us why this is so.

We must remember that although this is a chapter dealing with holiness and yielding to God, Paul *still* does not tell us anything to do yet. Verse 2b of chapter 6 is not telling us what to do; it is telling us about what has happened to us. He says: *Such people as us, we who died to sin, how shall we still live in it* (Rom. 6:2b). The particular word he uses here is emphatic: 'Such people as us!' The apostle is emphasising what has happened to us.

What does it mean, 'We died to sin'? That is the best translation. The King James translation ('we are dead to sin') is misleading. It is not dealing with our present state ('we are dead'). It is not spotlighting the way we have been for a long time ('we have died'). It is dealing with an event that happened some time ago ('we died!'), a definite once-for-ever occurrence that happened on a single occasion. Most modern translations translate it that way. When the 'Revised King James' translation was produced they rightly changed it from 'we were dead' to 'we died'. The change was a good one. It is the tense often used when talking about Jesus' death. In Romans there are times when the death of Jesus is referred to and this particular tense is used. Romans 5:6, 'Christ died'. Romans 5:8, 'Christ died'. Romans 8:34, 'It is Christ who died'. Romans 14:9, 'Christ both died and rose again'. Romans 14:15, 'Christ died'. Each of those verses uses the same simple past tense. It is the same tense used in Romans 6:2. The idea is that there was a definite time when something happened to us. 'We died!' What is this event and when did it happen and how did it happen?

We may think of it in a number of ways. (i) Think of it as ceasing to be 'in Adam'. Romans 5:12–21 told us that we were 'in Adam'. I sinned in Adam. I inherited a sinful nature in Adam. I fell subject to death in Adam. But I am no longer in Adam. I have died. The person I used to be has gone, and gone for ever.

Or (ii) think of it using the picture language of two kingdoms. It means that we have been transferred to the kingdom of grace. Colossians 1:13 tells us that we have been transferred out of the kingdom of darkness into the kingdom of Jesus. Darkness was my king. Sin and Satan was my king. But I have 'died' to that territory, that ruling authority over my life. It is not that sin does not exist. But I am not under its dominion.

Imagine that one day I am in India, driving at a lunatic speed along one of India's roads. Will the policemen of Kenya be coming after me? Will I be in trouble with the government of America? No, of course not. I am not in their kingdoms, their territories. I am currently in a different regime altogether. Now the same is true of the Christian. He has 'died' to the regime, the kingdom, the citizenship of sin. It is not that he cannot sin but he is not under the rule of sin.

(iii) Or focus on the word 'under'. The New Testament tells me that I am not 'under' law; I am 'under' grace. Equally I am not 'under' sin.

(iv) Or think of it in terms of the word 'rule' or 'reign'. Paul tells me 'death reigned' (Rom. 5:14, 17) and 'sin reigned in death' (Rom. 5:21). But now I have died to that. Now it is not sin that reigns. It is righteousness that reigns. Or I reign in righteousness. Or life reigns. Or grace reigns. Better still: Jesus reigns! I have 'died' to that phase of my existence in which sin and death reigned over me. This is not something I am trying to get to happen. It happened when I believed in Jesus. The reign of sin came to an end.

The key to Romans 6 is Romans 5:12–21. A death has taken place, a transfer. We are not the person we used to be. It *has* happened. It is not saying that the Christian *wants* to die to sin or that he is dying to sin *more and more*. True, it is possible to use this kind of language. We sometimes say, 'I am dying to self.' We mean that as our life goes on we are learning more and more to resist the selfishness and self-centredness that we find within ourselves. That is fine. And 'dying to self' in that sense is a good thing to do. But that is not what Paul is talking about here! It is *not* the way the word is being used in Romans 6:2. Here he is not talking about something we ought to do, or something that we hope will be progressively more true of us. What Paul is referring to here has been done. It is decisive. It is final. It is irreversible. It makes sin to be defeated. I have died. It has no claims as the ruling authority over my life.

BAPTISMS
(Romans 6:3)

The Christian has 'died to sin'. You could say that it happened two thousand years ago. Paul constantly refers to what happened when Jesus died. The Christian has died in Christ. We were placed into *His* death. We were buried when He was buried (Rom. 6:4). I was 'made alive together with Christ' (Eph. 2:5). I have been 'raised . . . in Christ Jesus' (Eph. 2:6), 'raised together with Christ' (Col. 3:1). When did this happen? At the time Jesus died, I died.

Yet this became a reality at the time I was converted to Jesus Christ. The Holy Spirit took hold of me and placed me into Jesus Christ. I got joined on to Jesus, united to the Son of God. At that point I was given the power of Jesus to resist sin. It has happened already. I have died to sin. I have been taken out of sin's realm. Sin still exists, the devil still exists. I can still be attacked. But I do not belong to sin's realm. The same power that raised Jesus from the dead is flowing in me. Why should I sin? It does not make sense, it is illogical. I do not belong to sin's kingdom. When I do sin it is going against everything God has done for me. I get no blessing from it. It is not necessary, since I am alive and risen in Christ. I am capable of resisting it since Christ is alive in me. Shall I go on in sin? No, don't be so illogical! I have been released from sin and placed under God's grace. I have died to sin.

How did this 'dying to sin' take place? It happened because we were placed into Jesus Christ. *Or do you not know that such people as us, we who were baptised into Christ Jesus, it was into His death that we were baptised* (Rom. 6:3).

Again he uses this emphatic word, already used in Romans 6:2, 'such people as us!'. He is emphasising something that happened to us, something that makes us who and what we are. It simply means that we were placed 'into Christ' by the Holy Spirit.

Paul uses the Greek word 'baptised'. Many assume that

because he uses the Greek word 'baptised' he is using the word in a technical sense and referring to water-baptism. Personally I do not think that what he says is referring to water-baptism at all. The word 'baptism' is a Greek word. In a Greek dictionary it appears as *baptiso*. Any Greek dictionary will have it, whether it is a dictionary of classical Greek or of the Greek that was the language of the New Testament or of modern Greek. It is a very ordinary word. It means to 'dip' or 'immerse' or to be placed down into something. It is a pity that translators use the Greek word 'baptise'. That is not really a translation at all. It is simply using the Greek word! If it were really put into English a word like 'dip' or 'place' or 'put in' or 'immerse' would be used.

There are actually four ways in the New Testament in which this Greek word is used.

1. *The word is most well-known in connection with water baptism.* When people came to faith in Jesus (in New Testament times) they expressed their faith in a little ceremony in which they were 'immersed' or 'dipped' into water.

2. *The same word is used in connection with our being put through the experience of suffering.* On one occasion James and John approached Jesus and asked that when He came into His kingdom they should be rulers with Him. Jesus replied: 'Yes, you can rule with me but the kind of kingdom you are thinking of involves suffering. Are you able to be baptised with the baptism that I shall be baptised with?' Jesus clearly refers to an immersion into intense suffering.

3. A third way in which this word is used is in connection with *the outpouring or 'baptism' with the Holy Spirit.* A study of these passages and a few comparisons will show that this is something that Jesus does. He 'pours out' the Spirit on the believer. He immerses or baptises the believer with the Holy Spirit.

4. The New Testament also says that at the time of our first faith in Jesus *the Holy Spirit places us into Christ and into the body of Christ the church.* A study of the passages that use the word in this way will show that this is something that the Holy Spirit does. It is this that is surely the matter referred to in Romans 6:3. It is a work in which the Spirit baptises us into Christ and places the believer into close union with Him. The idea is found in 1 Corinthians 12:13, Galatians 3:27, Ephesians 4:5, Colossians 2:12 and our verse here in Romans 6:3. They all refer to the same spiritual event and so each one helps us to

understand the others. These passages are often thought to refer to water-baptism, but in my opinion there is no connection except that they happen to use the flexible and untechnical word 'baptise' or 'immerse'.

This work of the Holy Spirit placing me into Christ is the secret of my being a new person in Jesus. It is like a limb being united to a body (1 Cor. 12:12–13). It is like a branch being tightly fused into the trunk of a tree (John 15:5). It is like the unity between husband and wife when they become one flesh, a kind of unity of the personalities seems to take place (Eph. 5:29–32). This unity with Christ breaks the power of sin. How can I sin? I have died to sin. I have been placed into union with Jesus by the Holy Spirit!

IMMERSED INTO CHRIST
(Romans 6:3–4)

There are several major differences between water baptism and the Spirit's placing us into Christ. The greatest difference is in effectiveness. Water baptism does not in and of itself effect anything. It is a symbol of God's having already washed us from sin. People can be saved and filled with the Holy Spirit before being water-baptised, as Acts chapter 10 shows. If for some reason the people of Acts 10 had never been water-baptised they would still have been saved and filled with the Spirit. Water baptism is not in itself the conveyer of salvation or of the Spirit.

Admittedly, when faith is active as it should be when we are baptised, powerful and wonderful things can happen. Demons may leave the person being baptised, healings may take place, people may speak in tongues, prophecies may be given, and if the person being water-baptised has not received the experience of powerfully and consciously receiving the Spirit this may well take place as he is being water-baptised. Acts 2:38 promised precisely that to the new converts on the day of Pentecost. Often in water baptism where the Spirit is working powerfully people 'receive the Spirit' visibly and obviously. Water-baptism may certainly be a 'means of grace' in this sense, where the Spirit is at work and people are expecting blessings from God.

But it is not that the water is doing anything. It is simply that faith is present and God blesses faith. These blessings can be present when there is no water at all. And genuine Christian water baptism can take place without there being any 'phenomena' at all. Water baptism does not in itself effect anything.

But the Spirit's baptising us into Christ and into the body of Christ is a different matter altogether. There the Spirit Himself powerfully, irresistibly, effectively, inevitably, places us into Christ and into the body of Christ. The Spirit 'puts' or 'places' or 'immerses' us into Christ and into His body the church. With 100% certainty and effectiveness the Spirit does this work.

It is this part of our conversion, this 'placing' of us into Christ by the Holy Spirit that breaks the power of sin, transfers us into a new kingdom, secures that we are 'in Christ'. This is the event which in and of itself means that we have 'died to sin'. There are five places in the New Testament where this is described and the word 'baptised' is used. I do not think it refers to the ceremony of water baptism. It refers to a hidden, secret and powerfully effective work of the Holy Spirit.

Consider Ephesians 4:5. Paul is dealing with seven items that inevitably, irrefutably, irresistibly, inexorably unite the church of Jesus Christ and guarantee its unity. There is one body. That is why the church is one. There is one faith. That is why the church is guaranteed to be one. There is one Father, one Lord, one Spirit. The oneness of the threefold God guarantees the oneness of the church. There is one hope. All Christians have a common destiny. This guarantees and secures their unity. In this connection Paul says, 'There is one baptism.' What sort of baptism might this be? Does water baptism powerfully and irresistibly guarantee the unity of the church? Surely not. Does the baptism with the Spirit bring about unity? It has a tendency that way but can also be a matter of division! The thing that secures and in and of itself guarantees the unity of the church is the fact of the Spirit's placing us into the body of Christ. This is not water baptism. It is the effective placing of the believer into Christ and into the body of Christ. The thought is similar in 1 Corinthians 12:13, Galatians 3:27 and Colossians 2:12, although this is not the place to study them in detail. There are other differences between this 'baptism into Christ' and water baptism. In water baptism a human being does the baptising. In baptism into Christ the Spirit is the exclusive agent. No human agency is involved. It is exclusively a divine act. In the one case the immersion is into water; in the other case the Spirit immerses or places us into Christ.

This baptism by the Spirit into Christ and into the body of Christ is also distinct from what is commonly called the 'baptism with the Spirit'. The agent is different. Christ baptises with the Spirit; the Spirit baptises into Christ. The experience is different. Baptism into Christ is not an emotional experience. It has to be 'believed' or known by pure faith or 'reckoned'. But the baptism with the Spirit is vibrantly experiential. It is consciously known by the person receiving the Spirit and by others around him as well.

It is the Spirit's placing us into Christ that gives rise to a new possibility in our lives. *We have been buried therefore with Him through this being placed into this death of His, so that as Christ was raised from the dead through the glory of the Father, so also we might walk in newness of life* (Rom. 6:4). Something has happened to us 'in order that we may walk in newness of life'. This 'being placed into Christ' and therefore 'dying to sin' is the event in our lives that makes it possible to walk in newness of life and greatly encourages our doing so—as long as we know by faith that we have indeed died to sin. We are not yet looking at the new behaviour. Rather we are looking at what underlies it, what makes it possible. All Christians have died to sin. It is an event that has already taken place in the lives of all believers, by union with Jesus Christ.

A NEW POSSIBILITY
(Romans 6:4)

Everything God has done for us is designed to bring us out of sinful ways. At our very first point of trusting in Jesus we undergo a transfer of kingdoms and we die to sin. In terms of our position we undergo a great change. We are no longer in Adam; we have a position in Christ and under His grace. This removes us from the kingdom of sin. We die to sin once and forever.

Paul is working out what this means. We have been placed into the whole of Christ's story. We died with Christ. We were buried with Christ. We were 'quickened' (that is, given life) with Christ, we were raised with Christ. We have ascended with Christ. We are seated in the heavenly places with Christ. His story is my story. What happened to Him happened to me. My life is 'hid with Christ'. I have a new identity, I think about myself in an entirely new way, always in relation to Christ.

What Paul is doing in Romans 6:3–11 is this. He is insisting that if I have been placed into Christ, I have been placed into all the different aspects of the matter. I have died. I have been buried. I have been spiritually raised, and shall be physically raised in Christ. Paul wants us to see these different aspects of our being united to Jesus. Don't you know, he says, that if you have been placed into this unity with Christ, then one part of the matter is that you have been placed into His death? We have died in Christ. This is just one of the aspects of our total union with Christ. Paul says in effect, 'Such people as us have been placed into union with Christ Jesus as a whole, it means that amongst other things it is into His death that we have been placed.' This means that we have been removed from the kingdom of sin.

Romans 6:4 develops the matter further. *We have been buried therefore with Him through this being placed into this death of His, so that as Christ was raised from the dead through the glory of the*

Father, so also we might walk in newness of life. Let us look at the main points of the verse.

1. I have not only died in Christ, I have also been buried in Christ. What is burial? It is the last thing that happens in this world to a person that has died. You do not bury someone until you are certain they have died. If there is any doubt, you wait. You only bury the body when you are 100% certain that a death has truly taken place.

So it was with Jesus. They were utterly certain they had killed him. They came to make doubly sure and pierced His side with the spear. Then He was buried and they thought they had got rid of Him for ever. 'He is dead and buried,' they said. The burial was the assurance and public declaration that He had died.

But I am 'in Christ'. What has happened to Him has happened to me. It has happened to me because it first happened to Him. The old 'me' was placed in a tomb. Not only did I die in Christ, my death in Christ is so thorough, so complete that my remains were put in a tomb. The old 'me' has disappeared out of view, out of consideration. I am not in the kingdom of sin, just as a skeleton in a tomb has finished with this world.

2. This total burial of what I was took place through my dying in Christ. Death leads to burial.

3. Christ was raised by the glory of the Father, that is, by the Father's glorious power. I am in Christ, so I have been raised to new life in Christ. This is clearly stated in verse 5. But it is assumed even in verse 4.

4. Because of my position as someone raised in Christ, I am able to walk in newness of life. At this point Paul comes to deal with the possibility of my actually living a godly life. So far Paul has only been referring to my position, my new status and kingdom. Now he deals with the new possibility that this gives rise to in me. It is 'so we might walk in newness of life'. I am actually able to do it. To walk! To go through life steadily, step by step, with regularity and persistence. I am able to live a life of Christlikeness, purity, dedication, assurance, obedience, graciousness, endurance, consecration, enjoying the liberty of the Spirit, walking in the sight of God, living for God's glory, loving everyone everywhere. The glory of the Father, the greatest display of power that the universe has ever seen, was put forth to raise Christ from the dead. But that greatest display of glorious

power at one and the same time raised me up. As the Father put Jesus into a new kingdom and realm, so He put me into a new kingdom and realm. I am able to be a new person, to believe where I used to doubt, to rejoice where I used to complain, to act with energy where I used to be indolent, to trust in Jesus' blood where I used to trust in myself, to obey the Spirit where I used to resist the Spirit. To think as the Spirit thinks, to do what He says I am to do, to go where He says I am to go, to give when He says to give, to pray when He says 'Pray'. Newness of life! It is wonderful!

7

RISEN WITH CHRIST
(Romans 6:5)

Paul has told us that we are 'placed' (or 'baptised') into Christ. Now he uses a different word, 'fused together'. Newness of life is possible. *For if we have become united with the likeness of His death, it is certain we shall also be united with the likeness of His resurrection* (Romans 6:5). The word 'united' is the word that (in the ancient world) would be used when a bone was broken and then as it healed the two ends of the bone were fused together. The Christian is 'fused together' with the likeness of Jesus' death and resurrection. He uses the word 'likeness' because we did not exactly go through every stage of Jesus' experience. We do not, for example, suffer literally as He did. Our resurrection in Christ is not witnessed by Roman soldiers. We die and rise again in the *likeness* of what happened to Him.

Some think Paul refers to the final resurrection, because it says *'shall* be' and *'shall* live' (verse 8). But no. Our future physical resurrection is part of it, but here Paul is answering the question about whether grace encourages a godly life. Remember the starting-point of the whole section. 'Are we to continue in sin . . . ?' In verse 4 we are told we are able to 'walk in newness of life'. This is not referring to the final resurrection. We 'shall live' the risen life now! Our position as risen in Christ enables us to walk in newness of life in this world. In verse 6 again he says that this matter of 'living' because we are raised in Christ is 'so that we might no longer serve sin'. He is not thinking only about the distant future; he is thinking also about the immediate future. A better way of taking 'shall be' and 'shall live' is this. It is a future that expresses certainty. 'If we have become united with the likeness of His death, we *shall*—for certain—also be united with the likeness of his resurrection.' It is expressing what is true of us now and in the *immediate* future.

I have been placed into *all* the different aspects of the matter. I have not only died in Christ, I have also been buried in

Christ. Now, he says, I have been also raised to new life in Christ. This is why I am able to walk in newness of life.

Being risen with Christ is a position of optimism and joy. If all the glorious power that raised Jesus from the dead is working in me, then I can be quite confident that I am able to deal with sin. I am able to put it down. I am able to positively live the life of love and holiness that God is calling me to. I am certain of victory over particular battles because the whole war has been won. For I am risen for ever with the resurrection-life of Jesus. Our greatest need is a sense of encouragement and assurance. We can do anything if we feel we can do it. We can do very little when we feel discouraged. Most Christians are prone to sin because they feel so weak and discouraged. But there is nothing more encouraging than to take it by faith that I am risen with Christ!

It is a position I take hold of in sheer faith. It is not that I necessarily 'feel' very risen with Christ. I am being asked to believe it as a sheer fact. When I believed in Jesus I was at that moment united by the Holy Spirit to Jesus and to the story of the events that happened to Him. It is a fact that I am risen with Christ and alive unto God. But I have to believe it as a sheer, plain, stark, fact. If I start believing it I shall then experience it. I take it purely on the basis of God's Word that I am risen with Christ. If I view myself as a person alive from the dead and no longer under sin's dominion, and start living with this as a basic conviction of my life, I shall then feel and notice practically the fact that I am a new person. It will be realised in my life. But it is a position of faith and I do not necessarily feel it.

Have you ever noticed that resurrection songs can be sung about Jesus, but they can also be sung about ourselves? We may sing:

Alive, alive, alive for evermore
My Jesus is alive, alive for evermore
Alive, alive, alive for evermore
My Jesus is alive.

But if I am united to Jesus and am risen from the dead in Jesus, then I can sing that song about myself.

Alive, alive, alive for evermore
I know that I'm alive, alive for evermore

Alive, alive, alive for evermore
I know that I'm alive.

Being risen with Christ is the basis of my being open to God. A dead person cannot be reasoned with, cannot be persuaded, cannot be motivated, cannot be moved with excitement. But I am risen with Christ, I am alive! So the channels of communication between me and God are open.

Sin attacks me and harasses me. But it is only a nuisance. It really has no power. I grasp hold of my position as a person risen from the dead. I hold my head up high with optimism and expectancy. I do not let any feelings of discouragement knock me over. And I move forward with God living the positive life of holiness, love, purity, joy, service. Nothing can stop me. I am alive. I can walk in newness of life.

8

THE OLD SELF CRUCIFIED
(Romans 6:6a)

Another way of putting the points Paul has made now comes in verse 6. *Know this: our old person was crucified with Him . . .* (The first word may be translated 'Knowing', but it can also have the force of a command.)

What is the 'old man' or 'old person' or 'old self'? It is everything that I was in Adam. It is not dealing with a part of me, such as 'the flesh'. That is not the point here. Paul is simply pursuing the thoughts of Romans 6:1–5. I died in Christ. The *entire person* was once united to Adam, but that phase of my life is finished. The person I once was died; he no longer exists. I am a new person altogether. I could translate it: 'The person I used to be was crucified with Christ', or 'My former self was crucified with Christ.'

If my former self was crucified with Christ, I do not have to try to get the old 'me' crucified. I do not have to try to mortify 'me'. 'I' was crucified with Christ. The person I was has gone, has ceased to exist in this world at all. Paul is not thinking of a process. He is thinking of a once-and-for-ever event.

Again we must remind ourselves that Paul has not yet come to the point where he is telling us to do anything. It is a great mistake to try to do anything in the Christian life *before* we realise what has been done to us and what has happened to us.

Your former self has gone altogether. This is very liberating and encouraging. The Christian is not simply adjusting his old life, or making a few modifications, or adding a bit of religion. What happened to you when you believed in Jesus is an amazing thing. At the point where you believed, you were fused and welded and locked into Jesus. His crucifixion became your crucifixion. And in the fraction of a second (when you believed in Jesus), your former self ceased to exist. Your former self was crucified when Jesus died for the human race upon the cross. And it became a fact in your history the moment you believed in Jesus. Don't think you have to modify what you used to be. The *person* you used to be has gone altogether. You are a new person.

In Colossians we have similar teaching. 'Tell no lies one to another,' says Paul, 'because you have put off the old person with its practices and you have put on the new person who is being renewed after the Creator's image' (Col. 3:9, 10). The passage is similar except that whereas in Romans 6 the dying of the old person is something that the Holy Spirit does, something that happens to us, in Colossians the emphasis is more on what we did at the time we believed. We believed. And in so doing we voluntarily put off our old style of living. God made us new people; the old person ceased to exist (so far as our position was concerned). And then we doubly got rid of him by our repenting of sin and abandoning the old lifestyle. The old person has been doubly got rid of. By God in making us new people, risen in Christ. By ourselves, in our throwing off the old lifestyle.

Ephesians 4:22–24 is more difficult because it has been translated in different ways. It is sometimes translated as a series of commands: 'Put off the old person . . . Put on the new person.' If this is correct the thought goes like this. 'You are *not* your old person. That has ceased to exist. So get rid of the *behaviour* which comes from your old life.' That is a possible way of taking it. But actually it is more likely that Ephesians 4:22–24 contains not commands but statements. 'You were taught in such a way (at the time of your conversion) with regard to your former way of life, that you put off your old self . . . and you put on the new self . . . .' The teaching is the same as in Colossians 3. The Christian has decisively broken off from his old life by trusting in Jesus Christ. At that point of conversion the Spirit baptises us into Jesus and our old life was gone in that instant! We ourselves put off the 'old self' so far as our behaviour is concerned. It does not mean that our *behaviour* was completely changed in a flash; we have to go on being renewed in the spirit of our minds. But our basic *position* was completely changed in a flash. Distinguish between position and behaviour. Romans 6 deals with position and what God does; Colossians and Ephesians deal with behaviour and what we do.

According to Romans 6, there is a *first* result of this, and there is a *second* result. The immediate result is this: the body of sin is made powerless. The further result is 'so that we might no longer serve sin'.

The way to understand this section is to realise that Paul is making a sharp distinction between our true selves and our bodies. There is a difference between 'me' and 'my body'. I know my body is part of me! But it is a part of me that is still fallen, still with strong sinful tendencies in it. When my body is fully and perfectly redeemed I shall never sin again. But meanwhile my body is the channel along which sin attacks me. So I must distinguish between the 'me' who does not want to sin, and the fact that sin attacks me through the body. I disassociate myself from the sinfulness that attacks me through the body. I say to myself, I know that sin attacks me through my fallen body but 'I' have died to sin. 'I' am in the kingdom of grace. 'I' can put down this nuisance called sin, and I will!

9

FREEDOM FROM SIN
(Romans 6:6b)

Paul tells us what happens because the 'old person' was crucified. It was *in order that the body of sin might be made powerless so that we might no longer serve sin*. The body of sin is a reference to the literal body. It is called the body *of sin*, because sin attacks me through the body. It is not the 'old person'. For it would not make sense to say 'our old person was crucified with Him, in order that our old person might be made powerless'. It would be saying the same thing twice!

We need to keep clear in our minds the meaning of some New Testament terms. (1) The *old self* or *old person* is 'old' in the sense that it was in Adam, the old world that is going to pass away completely in Jesus. We are delivered from it already and are 'new' people in Jesus and alive to God. The old person is everything that I was in Adam. It has ceased altogether.

(2) The *body of sin* is my body itself. The reason why it is called the 'body of sin' is that sin uses it. It is the part of my total person that is unredeemed. Sin attacks me because my body is still mortal, still fallen.

(3) Then there is the word *flesh* that Paul uses later. The 'body of sin' is more or less the same as 'the flesh'. Paul uses the two almost interchangeably in Romans 8:12–13. The word flesh can mean just 'human nature' without stressing sinfulness. (For example, 'The Word became flesh' means that Jesus became a real human being. It does not mean He became sinful.) But often the word *flesh* means the sinful side of my nature. In this sense it is the same as the 'body of sin'. It is not the whole of me; it is a part of me. It is the overhang of my old life. It is the tug and pull towards sin that comes from the fact that I still have a mortal body. The New International Version translates 'flesh' as 'sinful nature'. This could be misleading. It is not the whole of my nature. It is rather the sinful hangover. So the 'flesh' is the sinful part of my existence now. The 'old person' has gone, but the

flesh has not. Once the flesh ruled me. Now the flesh does not rule me, because I am in Christ. But it is still present as a problem, as a nuisance. The 'flesh' is still there and still resists the Holy Spirit. But it must be remembered that the 'flesh' is only a part of me, it is that tendency in me to pull away from true spirituality. But it is not the whole of me, not my whole position. 'I'—my position as a whole—am in Christ and have died to sin. These distinct ideas must be kept clear in our minds, otherwise we shall be confused.

Romans 6:6 says that this 'body of sin' or tendency that I have to sin is stripped of its power because I have died to sin and have become alive to God. The 'flesh' or 'body of sin' is still there but it is 'stripped of its power'. The body of sin, the flesh, the sinful nature is nullified, stripped of its power, set aside, rendered powerless. It is similar to what is said about the devil in Hebrews 2:14, which speaks of Jesus 'destroying the power of the devil'. The power of the sinfulness of the body has been similarly 'destroyed'. It has not been totally annihilated but it has been drastically reduced in power. It can no longer lord it over us, no longer be a tyrant demanding that we obey its demands.

I have not used the word 'nature'. It is a slightly confusing word. Some people use it for the *whole* position in which the Christian finds himself. Others use it to translate the 'flesh' which is only a side of what I am. Actually the Greek word for 'nature' does not occur often in the New Testament but the New International Version translates the Greek word for 'flesh' by 'sinful nature'. But it must be remembered that the 'flesh' is only a part of me, it is that tendency in me to pull away from true spirituality. But it is not the whole of me, not my whole position. 'I'—my position as a whole—am in Christ and have died to sin.

According to Paul I am able to live a new life. In verse 4 he said I can 'walk in newness of life'. Now in verse 6 he says the body of sin is made powerless and I am able to break free from the habits of sin and no longer serve them.

It is also a mistake to talk as if the Christian has *now* an old self and a new self at the same time. People often talk this way but it is not quite right. True, the Christian has 'the flesh' and the Holy Spirit at the same time. But this is not to say that he has an 'old self' and 'new self' at the same time. The 'old self' is the total person enslaved by sin. That person has gone! Romans 6:6 is utterly clear at this point. The old person was crucified.

We are no longer the old selves that we used to be. Only the remaining bits of behaviour are left and we are to put them off; but the old self ('me', enslaved to sin) has gone already! The old self is the un-saved self; the new self is the converted self, the new 'me'. I am not saved and unsaved at the same time! The unconverted 'me' has gone; I am a new 'me'.

10

THE GREAT VICTORY
(Romans 6:6b—7)

The letter to the Romans has much to say about the body. The 'body of sin' is the body itself as it is being used by sin. There are six things we ought to bear in mind.

1. *The body is not evil in itself.* Christ had a body, and the body was part of God's original creation which was 'very good' (Gen. 1:31). It is meant to glorify God (1 Cor. 6:60) and God will bring it to full health and glory eventually (Rom. 8:23).

2. *However the body is not yet redeemed.* It is a 'body of humiliation' (Phil. 3:21), and is an old clay pot (2 Cor. 4:7, 10). It is 'wasting away' (2 Cor. 4:16).

3. To understand Romans 6 we must realise that *although the body is not sinful itself it is used by sin.* This is why it is called a 'body of sin' (Rom. 6:6), and a mortal body (Rom. 6:12), a 'body of death' (Rom. 7:24). 'The body is dead,' says Romans 8:10.

4. But *we have died and been buried with Christ.* This means that the 'body of sin'—the body that we battle with because it is the avenue along which we can be tempted—is stripped of its power. We are able not to let sin reign in our mortal bodies (Rom. 6:12) and can mortify the deeds of the body (Rom. 8:13) and can discipline the body (1 Cor. 9:27).

5. More than that *we are to positively put the limbs of our bodies at the disposal of God.* We 'present our bodies' a living sacrifice (Rom. 12:1) and remember they are temples of the Holy Spirit (1 Cor. 6:20). We are to keep them holy (1 Cor. 7:34) and must yield each member or part to God (Rom. 6:15–23).

6. One day *our bodies will be raised by Jesus* (1 Cor. 6:13–14). The body will be redeemed (Rom. 8:23); the Spirit will give them final life and resurrection (Rom. 8:11). It is this that we are looking for and waiting for (Rom. 8:23). The resurrection body will not be exactly identical to the present body, although there will be a similarity. We shall be recognisable in glory. It will be a new glorious body (1 Cor. 15:43–44; Phil. 3:21) and the holiness

we have reached while here on earth will be for ever observable in our glorified shining exalted bodies in the new heavens and new earth in which righteousness will dwell.

In verse 7 he explains what he has said in Romans 6:6. We are no longer enslaved to sin, *For he that has died is legally released from sin.* The word 'legally released' here is the same as the word translated 'justified'. But it has a special meaning here, and does not mean 'justified' in the way the word is used in Romans 3:24. (It is not true that 'he that has died' is *justified*. The opposite is true: he that is justified has died to sin. 'Justified' has a different meaning here and should be translated with a different word, like 'released'.) The King James Version translates 'freed', which is good but it must be remembered that the word has a *legal* atmosphere to it. It means *legally* released, righteously released.

This is the wonderful position the Christian is in. We need to pray for a revelation of the Holy Spirit. It is possible to state all this as doctrine but somehow not see it. When we see it—by the Spirit—it is the most wonderful thing imaginable. At the moment we are only looking at the negative, the way I have been released. Verses 8–10 go on to expand in detail what we have been *into* and *for*, the *positive* new life. But even the negative is wonderful! The old 'me' has gone. Paul actually says that sin is not dwelling in *me* at all. This seems a staggering thing to say. Yet it is precisely what Paul does say and he says it again in Romans 7:23 where he does not say 'Sin dwells in me' but 'Sin dwells in my members.' Sin does not dwell in 'me'. This is an amazing thing to say and I suppose it could be misunderstood and misused. Paul is certainly not saying that when we sin God does not notice. Nor is he saying that it is impossible for the Christian to sin, or anything like that. But he is stating clearly precisely what the problem is. Sin does not dwell in 'me'. 'We' are no longer enslaved to sin. The 'us' that once existed under the domination of sin has ceased. And there is now a new 'us', a new 'me'. Sin only dwells in my 'body' it does not dwell in me. When my body is finally redeemed it will not even dwell in my body. It will not be anywhere near me at all, and in that day I shall be beyond temptation. It will be impossible for me to sin once I have my resurrection body.

But even now, although it is possible for me to sin, because I still live with my mortal body, yet 'I' am risen with Christ. 'I' am in control. 'I' am in a position in Christ where I can put down the sinful inclinations that come to me through the body. Sin is no longer in me, it is in my members only. It is what Martyn Lloyd-Jones called 'the most liberating thing you have ever heard'! Released from sin! Righteously! Legally! Permanently! Sin will not rule over me. I just have a few little challenges from an enemy that has been decisively cast out of my life and can only harass me through the body. The greatest victory has been won.

ASSURANCE OF NEW LIFE
(Romans 6:8–9)

We must follow Paul's argument. In Romans 6:1–2a Paul asked a question (Can we go on in sin?) and answered it (No!). Then he told us why we can't go on in sin. We have died to sin (6:2b).

Romans 6:3–5 began to develop the point. We were fused into Jesus' death (6:3) and that involves being fused into Jesus' burial and walking in newness of life (6:4). A vital statement came in verse 5. If we have been united with Jesus in His death we shall be united with Jesus in His resurrection. Paul is now amplifying verse 5. Romans 6:6–7 enlarges the negative side, the bit about having died to Christ. Now in Romans 6:8–10 Paul will develop the thought about being risen with Christ.

Once again Paul puts the fact before us: 'we died with Christ.' He has used various phrases, 'we died to sin' (6:2), 'we were placed into His death' (6:3), 'we have become united with the likeness of His death' (6:5), 'our old person was crucified' (6:6). Now we have another expression. He is simply repeating his teaching using different phrases.

Once again he emphasises the two sides to the matter. We are delivered from the past; an inseparable part of the same event is the fact that we are brought into this risen life in Jesus in the present life we are living. He says *And if we died with Christ we believe that we shall also live with Him.* Paul implies that we find it easier to believe we have died with Christ than to believe we have risen with Christ. Why is this? It is because we get discouraged by our feelings of weakness. We are not so sure that we are risen with Christ. But Paul says, they are two sides of the same event. If we died with Christ, we believe that we *shall* also live with Him.

He says 'we believe' this. It is an act of faith, something to be received on the basis of God's word. Satan loves to discourage us and plays upon the feeling we have that we are not very strong in Jesus. But Paul refuses to allow discouragement over this matter. We believe it, he says.

Many have jumped to the conclusion that Paul is referring *only* to the final resurrection, because it says '*shall* live'. But Paul is mainly answering the question about whether grace encourages a godly life. He must be dealing with the Christian's immediately being alive in Christ.

Yet it includes the long-distance future as well. It stretches out into eternity because it goes on to say that we believe we shall live with Christ, *knowing that Christ having been raised from the dead does not die any more, death no longer lords it over Him.* So the thought reaches into eternity. Christ shall never die. The believer is in Christ. So the believer will never die.

Paul wants to underline the certainty of it. 'We believe that we *shall* also live with Him.' Our having died with Christ logically leads to the fact that we shall live with Him. We have been united into the whole of the story of Jesus, as we have seen. We have been 'made to sit with Christ in the heavenly places' (Eph. 2:4).

In verse 9, the word 'knowing' reinforces 'we believe' (verse 8). We believe something about ourselves because we *know* something about Christ. We can be certain about ourselves because we are certain about Jesus.

The Christian is to come to a great certainty about himself or herself. We are totally delivered from the realm of spiritual death and darkness. The *dominion* of death is finished for Jesus, and therefore finished for the Christian who is 'in Christ'. Our spiritual death, at the time when we were people cut off from God, has been reversed. We know God. We are alive. Our physical death is not really death at all. 'Whoever lives—that is, has this resurrection life of Jesus—and believes in me shall never die,' says Jesus (John 11:26). The physical decay of our body and its end in what we call 'death' is not really death at all. It is not the wages of sin. The Christian's death is simply a gateway into paradise. We shall never come 'under' death. We are delivered from it now. And we shall be delivered from it even when this stage of our life on planet earth comes to an end.

It is a permanent deliverance. Jesus will never go back, never fall out of heaven. We are in Jesus. No foe can take us out of our position in Christ.

How then do we get to this assurance? By our certainty about Jesus. This is the way Christian assurance works. We might feel very uncertain about ourselves, but assurance comes by our looking to Christ. If we have a sure and certain knowledge about Jesus we may come to have a sure faith about ourselves. A true Christian often feels uncertain about himself, but he does not feel uncertain about Jesus. 'Faith is assurance . . . ' (Heb. 11:1) but it is not self-assurance. It is the assurance that comes simply by the Spirit when He shows us Jesus as Saviour, Lord, Intercessor, King. But if we are sure about Him we can immediately be sure about ourselves. My assurance comes because I am sure about Him. Paul is being logical: 'if we died with Christ' (as we have) then we can go a stage further: 'we believe that we shall also live with Him'. Where does this belief come from? It comes because we *know* 'that Christ having been raised from the dead does not die any more' and that 'death no longer lords it over Him'.

12

RECKONING
(Romans 6:10–11)

Paul continues to explain what it means to be united with Christ in His resurrection. He says, *For the death He died, He died to sin once, but the life He lives, He lives to God.*

He is referring to Jesus. Jesus died 'to sin'. It does not mean that He died 'for sin'. Nor does it mean that Jesus had any experience of sinning. For Jesus was sinless. Rather it means that Jesus came into the realm of sin. He came to deal with it. He came to take upon Himself the sorrows and temptations of sinners. There came a point where He was bearing the sins of the human race. He was doing what He was doing 'with respect to sin'. He died 'in the matter of sin'.

But when Jesus died He finished that stage of His ministry. He died to that realm of sin altogether. His time in the realm of sin had come to an end, so that He no longer belonged to it. He had fully borne and paid for all of the consequences of sin. Never again would He have to die again, or come under the weight of sin.

Then He was given new life. He was raised by the Father from the dead. Jesus was raised by a mighty act of power and was utterly delivered from the realm of the dead. He did not simply go back to His old position on earth. He kept on rising and was exalted and became the King of the universe.

Now He lives unto God. It means that He lives exclusively in the realm of God. He administers the Father's will. He is worshipped as the Son of God. He is in a position of supreme power, head over all things for His body, the church. He has the keys of death and Hades.

But the Christian is 'in Christ'. Christ is 'alive unto God', that is, living in the realm of the Father with all of the channels of communication open between Him and the Father. Then this is the precise position of the Christian! So the Christian is urged to grasp hold of the fact. *So also you are to reckon yourselves as dead to sin but alive to God in Christ Jesus.* Romans 6:11 is the first command in the letter to the Romans (or the second if Romans 6:6 is translated 'Know this . . . ').

In Romans 6 Paul begins with facts. He does not rush to tell us what to do. We are not ready to be told what to do until we know who we are and where we are. We are the children of God and we are risen with Christ. It is only when we have grasped hold of these things that Paul will tell us to deal with sin. More detailed instructions will wait even longer, until chapter 12.

Often people rush to urge men and women to live good lives. But Paul does not do that. He is not simply telling people to live godly lives. He first shows them the basis of their doing so. He wants us to see our position in Jesus first. We shall never live a godly life unless we are rejoicing. The joy of the Lord is our strength. And any kind of discouragement will be our weakness.

The secret of holiness is to come at it indirectly. If you walk up to the high demands of God and simply try to reach up to them you will fail miserably. No! Go back to the position you are in first. See that you have died to sin. See that sin is not in 'you', it is simply in the 'body of sin'. You have died to sin! And see that you are 'alive to God'.

What does it mean to 'reckon'? It means you grasp hold of what has happened to Jesus. Then it means that you realise that what is true of Him is true of you. He has died to this realm of sin; you have died to the realm of sin. He is living in a new realm in the presence of God; you are living in a new realm in the presence of God. The word 'you' is emphatic. Consider that you *yourselves* have finished with the realm of sin. It is not something I am trying to get to happen. It has happened already. I am not hoping it will be true. It is true! 'I', the inner 'me', 'I' in my personality have died to sin, in the sense that I am not in its kingdom and it does not rule over me.

To 'reckon' does not mean to 'pretend'. We are not trying to pretend we are dead to sin when we know we are not! We *are* dead to sin. To 'reckon' is just to count upon what God says about us as being true. Paul has already talked about knowing (6:6, 9) and believing (6:8). Reckoning is a similar word. It does not mean struggling or trying to get something to happen. It simply means to grasp hold of what has happened, what is true of me. I am not trying to accomplish something; I am rather seeing what has been accomplished for me. I am not under sin, nor under law, nor under death. Instead I am alive unto God. I have access to Him. His life and energy are in me. I am reconciled to God. He does not condemn me or moralise me. This is no great struggle. I know, I believe, I reckon. I am in the kingdom of God's grace. I am not ruled over by sin. I am alive in the realm of the liveliness of the Son of God.

13

REFUSING SIN'S REIGN
(Romans 6:12)

Now at long last Paul issues a command for us to obey. If we have followed him this far we should be deeply reassured that we are able to put down the remaining sinful side of our being, the 'body of sin'. So now Paul tells us to do so. *Therefore —because of everything I have told you about yourselves—do not let sin reign in your mortal body so that you obey its desires.*

There are four entities mentioned in this verse: you, sin, your mortal body, and your body's desires. Let us think of each of them.

First, there is 'you'. Paul says 'You' are not to let sin reign in your mortal bodies. He has already told us about ourselves, who we are, what has happened to us. 'You,' says Paul, 'have died to sin and are alive to God.' You have all of the power of God working for you. Now, he says, I am asking you to do something. *You* do it. You are able to do so. Refuse to allow sin to reign in your bodies.

Secondly, there is sin. Although it is defeated, it is still there. The 'body of sin' has lost its power to domineer but it has not gone away.

Thirdly, there is 'your mortal bodies'. It is a phrase that reminds us of the teaching about our bodies. They are subject to decay and death. They are the channels along which sin comes at us.

Fourthly, there are the desires of the body. This does not refer only to *physical* sins such as immorality or gluttony or physical laziness. The point is that *all* sins come at us through the body. Jesus said that sin comes 'out of the heart' (Matt.15:18–19). But although sin comes out of our hearts, it is the fact that we are in mortal bodies that gives rise to the fact that sin still emerges from the heart.

So let us apply the command to ourselves. We notice, firstly, that *Christians are responsible for dealing with sins in their lives.* When the Christian believes, the Holy Spirit places him into Christ. The 'body of sin' loses its domineering power; the Christian is no longer the slave of sin. But this means that *we* are in the position to resist sin, and the apostle calls upon us to do so. God has placed us into Christ. Now we have some responsibility. It is not a matter of 'Let go and let God'. There is a hymn that asks 'What is there left for me to do?' and answers the question 'Simply to cease from struggling and strife', but this is not quite right. There is some striving to do in the Christian life. But we are striving from a standpoint of victory. We know that sin is not in me, it is only in my body. We know that we are in a position to put it down. We reckon—and this bit *is* without struggling and strife!—that we have died to sin and are alive unto God. Then we take up the challenge of dealing with the remaining sin we find in ourselves. It is not a matter of letting God do it or of handing it over to God. True, we are in a partnership. God is there. We are walking in fellowship with Jesus. We are full of trust in His help. But none of this means that we are handing over to God the responsibility for our growth.

This is the teaching of the entire Bible. We—yes 'we'—are not to let sin reign in our mortal bodies. We are to cleanse ourselves from every defilement of body and spirit, perfecting holiness in the fear of God (2 Cor. 7:1). We are to resist the devil (Jas. 4:7). The many commands of the New Testament are addressed to us. They are not simply topics for prayer or things that we give over to God. We are to 'Let love be genuine, hate what is evil, hold to what is good, love one another with the affections of brothers and sisters . . . ', and so on. These commands are addressed to us. 'If you know these things, *you* will be blessed if *you* do them.' But 'you' have to do them. The wonderful position of being 'in Christ' is *given* to us; we do not achieve it. After we see that 'we' have died to sin, the next step of dealing with the sins of the mortal body is our responsibility. We are put in a position of victory, and then we are to put down the sins that arise in our lives through the mortal body.

Secondly, notice that this means *we come to this task with a sense of victory.* We are only refusing to allow sin to reign in our mortal bodies. Paul did not say, 'Do not let sin reign in you.' We have seen there is a distinction in Romans 6 between 'us' and our bodies. Sin does not reign in us; it attacks us via the body only.

Paul uses the word 'mortal' bodies. Our bodies are the

part of us that are at present unredeemed. Paul uses this word partly to remind us where the problem comes from. It comes from this hang-over from our old life, the body of sin, the mortal body, the 'body of humiliation' (Phil. 3:21). He also uses it to remind us that the problem is only temporary. One day we shall have an immortal body, a body of glory. In that day we shall not have any problem with sin at all. Meanwhile we have to refuse to allow the defeated enemy, sin, to reign. We do not end with victory; we start with victory.

14

THE VICTORIOUS FIGHT
(Romans 6:12)

Paul says you are not to 'let sin reign in your mortal body so that you obey its desires'. We have died to sin, but this does not mean that sin has given up. We are in a kingdom of victory. We triumph over sin; it is already defeated. But although sin is a defeated enemy it will not surrender. It is going to fight back until the very end of our lives.

However this need not discourage. 'We'—our true personality—have died to sin. We are not under its dominion. So we can take up the battle with a sense of victory and fight a fight of faith against sin. And we can win the final struggle to put sin down. It is a struggle, but it is a struggle in a war that has already been won. Sin is not eradicated, but because we are not in its domain it is defeated.

This is the secret of the Christian life. It is first to know the teaching, to know your position as a victor and conqueror already. Then act in faith and joy and put down the sins that attack you. 'You shall know the truth and the truth shall set you free.' The truth that sets us free is supremely this truth that we are risen with Christ. If we grasp hold of it, it will liberate us indeed. Godly living is not just a matter of struggling to surrender. Nor is it the up-and-down business of repenting and failing and repenting and failing, and so on. If we grasp hold of 'the truth' and *then* act with power and confidence and triumph, we shall be free indeed.

This is something we have to do willingly and freely. God will not force us. Jesus said, 'If any person *wants* to come after me . . . '. He is looking for those who will see what their position is, and then make use of it, people who will make use of their triumphant situation.

We are responsible; we have a sense of victory. Then, thirdly, *this battle is largely a matter of handling our desires*. Paul talks about the 'your mortal body' and obeying 'its desires'.

The 'body of sin' attacks us in this way, by violently hurling or slyly infiltrating some pressure upon us that comes from our desires. Temptations come at us in the form of powerful yearning to do something, to have something, or to act in a certain way. When we are not being tempted we feel that we can resist anything that comes our way. But at the time of temptation itself we do not feel that way at all. We have strong desires. I am not referring simply to sexual desires, although these too may be one form in which powerful temptation may come. More powerful than sexual temptation is the yearning to speak when we know we ought not to speak.

So resisting sin means 'denying ourself', not just denying particular things to ourselves, but denying ourself (Matt. 16:24). It is a matter of recognising and resisting when these strong desires come. It is a matter of loving God so much that we keep away from areas of life where we know these desires are likely to be worse.

Do not obey the 'desires' of your mortal body. Recognise that they do not really belong to you, they belong to the 'body of sin' only, and one day you will be rid of that altogether. But you triumph over the mortal body even now!

'Mortify therefore your members which are upon the earth,' says Paul (Col. 3:5). This means that we recognise the way our 'members', the parts of our body, are used by sin to attack us. Then you put them to death. Strangle them. Best of all: starve them. Give them no food. Smother them: give them no breathing place. Cut off their lines of supply. Let them die of neglect. Paul mentions particular matters that might come to attack us. First: various forms of uncleanness. Then: evil desires and greed. He is thinking of things like excessive craving for luxury and wealth, the desire for prestige and success, vindictiveness, the zeal we have to prove that we are right, longing for physical pleasure of one kind or another.

Temptation is powerful and subtle. The way to withstand it is to be thoroughly committed to moving forward with God, *before* the temptation comes. These desires that come to us are 'deceitful' (Eph. 4:22). We are all so selfish, so blind to our self-centredness. We are always protecting ourselves, comforting ourselves. We are always imagining offences, always ready to think that we have been handled unfairly. These 'desires' in the physical parts of our nature cause such quarrellings. 'Where do wars and fightings among you come from? Do they not come from your desires that war in the members of your body?' (Jas. 4:1).

Face the seriousness of this matter. These desires 'make war against our lives' (1 Pet. 2:11). They also war against good relationships. All bad relationships, all quarrels between husbands and wives, all fights between politicians, all disputes between employers and workers, everything comes down to this. Our desires pull us in the direction of sin and selfishness.

We must take up the battle. We can do it. We are on the winning side. I must 'discipline my body and enslave it' (1 Cor. 9:27) bringing my body—not just my physical frame but all of the sins that flow from it—under control.

We can do it. We have died to sin. There is no need for sin to reign over our mortal bodies. They do not reign over 'us', and there is no need for sin to reign over the mortal body.

15

GIVING OURSELVES AWAY
(Romans 6:13)

Romans 6:12–13 moves from the negative (v. 12–13a) to the positive (v. 13b), from what we should not do to what we should do. The beginning of the verse continues the negative aspect. *And do not present your members as weapons of unrighteousness in the interests of sin.*

He tells us not to present our 'members' to the kingdom of sin. He is treating 'sin' as a kind of empire or kingdom. The 'members' of our body are its component parts, the particular units. It includes our limbs, our faculties, our brain and powers of thought and imagination, our emotions. We must not be guilty of mutiny against God's kingdom of grace. Sin is treachery; it is betrayal. It is like a citizen of a country working for an opposing power, handing over his resources to be used by the enemies of his nation.

If we do present the parts of our body to be used for unrighteousness, the kingdom of sin is carrying forward its programme. It is not 'harmless' or 'neutral'. If we present our faculties or limbs or brain or affections to unrighteousness, there will be some kind of consequence. The kingdom of sin will be carrying forward its programme through us. It is a serious matter to act 'in the interests of sin'. How often our emotions have been allowed to run wild in a way that serves the kingdom of sin. How often our imaginations have been misused. We have carelessly handed our faculties and limbs to God's enemy.

Paul loved to consciously give his body to God. When he was in prison he said 'Christ must be magnified in my body' (Phil. 1:20). His body must have been getting rough treatment at the time. But he was happy to have his very body at God's disposal. He told the Corinthians, 'Glorify God in your bodies' (1 Cor. 6:20).

It is giving the parts of our life to God that makes holiness practical. It is easy to think we are dedicated to God, when our tongues talk as they please, when our imaginations commit sins in the secret corners of our lives, when our temper or appetites have their way. True dedication to God gets down to details.

Paul does *not* say and never says, 'Do not yield *yourselves* to sin.' This makes sense because of what has been said in the earlier verses. 'We' cannot be given to sin! We—in our personalities—have died to sin and are in the kingdom of grace. It is impossible for us to yield *ourselves* to sin. Paul has already told us we are risen with Christ, never to go back again to the kingdom of sin. It is only our 'members' that are part of the 'mortal body' and can be misused in the interests of sin. It is only possible for us to yield our *members* to sin.

Paul follows the negative with the positive: *But present yourselves to God as people who are taken out of the realm of the dead and are living people, and present your members as weapons of righteousness to God.* We must not let sin reign in our bodies (6:12) and we must present our members as weapons of righteousness (v. 13a). But it is not enough to stop there. The New Testament presentation of the call to holiness always moves on to the positive. So Paul goes on, 'But present yourselves . . . '.

This is where holiness is reaching forward and taking great strides. It is one thing to hold ourselves back from sins. Even unconverted people sometimes do that for their own reasons. But the high point of Christian holiness comes when we are positively stretching forward to give ourselves to God and put every faculty we have at His disposal.

We begin by giving ourselves. We live no longer for ourselves but for Jesus who gave Himself for us. We do for Him in a small way what He did for us in a big way. We give ourselves away!

But to be practical we move on to the parts and the details. We yield the bits and pieces of our lives as well as the whole. We deceive ourselves otherwise. We abandon self-centredness. So often our Christian faith and interests are terribly self-centred. We are interested in 'my' prosperity or 'my' health or 'my' family. God is our Father; He has promised to meet all my needs. That is wonderful! The Christian life is wonderful!

Well, all of that is true. But true Christian holiness is advancing if there are other things on our hearts as well as our own needs. We are making progress when we have positively put ourselves at God's disposal to advance His kingdom.

Jesus lived this way. He could say 'My food is that I should do the will of Him who sent me' (John 4:34). Paul lived that way. He could say 'For me, to live is Christ' (Phil. 1:21).

Our giving of ourselves and our faculties to God in this way is only logical. We have been raised from the death of sin's kingdom. We are risen in Christ, 'people who are taken out of the realm of the dead and are living people'. It hardly makes sense to participate in a kingdom we have left and resist the kingdom we have joined. Christian godliness is patriotism towards a new kingdom, a new citizenship. We are alive! We are not just people following a religious routine. We are sharing in the triumph and kingship of Jesus. He is leading us through this world. Because He is alive, we are alive. We know what we are doing. We deliberately put ourselves and our weapons at the disposal of our King.

16

LIFE UNDER GOD'S GRACE
(Romans 6:14)

Paul gives a reason why we must give ourselves to God. It is the only sensible thing to do. *For sin shall not have dominion over you. For you are not under law but under grace* (Rom. 6:14).

One might have expected Paul to say, 'You are not under *sin* but under grace'. He could have said that. It would have been quite true and it would have fitted with everything he has said so far. But he changes the word.

Why does he say 'law' when we might have expected him to say 'sin'? Elsewhere Paul says, 'The strength of sin is the law.' Paul is approaching Romans chapter 7, where he will tell us that sin was strengthened by the attempt to deal with it by law-keeping. Actually you can make a thousand resolutions to keep the Mosaic law or any other codified law. All that happens is that we discover how strong sin is.

When we grasp what it is to live under God's grace, we shall find ourselves much stronger to resist sin. The opposite of grace is sin. But it is also true, that the opposite of grace is law, living by focusing on rules. To go back to the law is to go back to the flesh (Gal. 3:3).

I do not mean that the godly life cannot be put into principles and guidelines. It can. The New Testament is full of definite statements about what the godly life involves. But the commanding parts of the New Testament are not simply a law-book. They are putting into words what the leading of the Spirit is. They are not an exhaustive code of laws, but are the sweeping guidelines of what will be the leading of the Spirit. What is the difference? Following a law does not require personal fellowship. The large-scale principle of the Spirit's leading is precisely that, the guiding of our personal Friend and Counsellor the Spirit. The two are different in content (the Ten Commandments are less than 1% of 'the law' and the bulk of 'the law' we no longer keep at all). They are different in level (the

law of the Mosaic covenant is too low a level of godliness for the
Christian). They are different in accompanying power (for the
law provides no power but the Spirit places us in Christ and
continues to lead). They are different in motivation (the law
terrifies; the Spirit draws us in love as well as fear of grieving the
Spirit). They are different in availability of forgiveness (the law
did not forgive major sins; grace does). They are different in
level of success (the law fails; grace succeeds).

How does grace help us? Grace gives us a sure position.
We have been seeing it throughout Romans 6:1–13. Grace will do
whatever needs to be done. Do we need chastening to keep us in
the narrow way? The grace of God will provide it. The grace of
God will give us a sense of God's presence. The Lord will stand
by us in times of unusual trial. As our days are, so shall our
strength be. His grace will be sufficient for us.

The grace of God will work all things together for our
good. When we feel that things are going wrong, often it is the
grace of God getting things to go right in surprising ways.

The grace of God has a programme for our lives and for
the whole of the body of Christ, the church.

The grace of God will be abundant over us. The Bible
constantly talks of the 'exceeding riches of His grace' (Eph. 1:7;
2:7) and the 'unsearchable riches of Christ' (Eph. 3:8). It talks of
'grace upon grace' or one expression of grace after another. It
talks of God's manifold grace (1 Pet. 4:10) which means the many
varied ways in which God's grace shows itself to us and takes
care of us. This is what we are 'under'. Grace is a king—a
sovereign ruler over all our affairs.

I love to think of the surprising triumphs of grace. God's
grace has ways of twisting and turning things round so
unexpectedly. Think of the story of Moses' parents, and how
Moses' young life was threatened. 'All Israelite baby boys are to
be thrown into the Nile!' was Pharaoh's decree (Exod. 1:22). But
the grace of God was at work to protect Moses. His parents were
led to put him into the Nile in a basket. Pharaoh did not say you
couldn't use a basket! And then God steered that little basket
downstream until He brought it to the feet of Pharaoh's
daughter. So Moses' mother ended up getting a salary from the
palace to look after her own son. The amazing grace of God!

It is this that guarantees that we shall not be ruled by sin.
Again, it is a fact! Paul is not putting it to us as a duty or an
obligation or something he hopes to be true. He puts it as sheer

fact. Sin *shall not* have dominion over us. God's grace rules and reigns. God's grace is not a feeble little prop or comfort on offer. It is a mighty king, master, ruler. Sin shall not rule over us. Grace rules over us. It is a fact.

The greatest thing that grace does for us is to protect us. He who began a good work in us will go on performing until the day of Christ. God's grace will rescue us from every attack and bring us through to God's final heavenly kingdom. God's people shall never perish; no one shall snatch them from Jesus' hand. God is determined to bring us to holiness and to bring us to heaven. He will do it, but not by law. By grace.

17

ENSLAVED TO RIGHTEOUSNESS
(Romans 6:15–17)

Paul has a habit of going over the same ground twice. Romans 6:1–14 and Romans 6:15–23 deal cover the same theme.

So Romans 6:15–23 begins with the same question, more or less, as he asked in chapter 6, verse 1. *What then? Are we to sin because we are not under law but under grace?* Again he says, *May it not be* (Rom. 6:15)! He is coming back to the same subject matter again. Does grace encourage sin? No!

But now he comes at the matter more practically. He has told us about our position. Now he wants to practically urge us to make use of our position, to actually yield our members to God. He wants to show us that it is inevitable (but not automatic!) that we live a godly life. We *must* do so. We must face the fact and see that it is good sense to live a godly life, and get on with the task of co-operating with the Lord as He seeks to bless us.

First he says, *Do you not know that to whom you present yourselves as slaves for obedience, you are the slaves of the one whom you obey, whether of sin leading to death or of obedience leading to righteousness?* (Rom. 6:16) Any kind of regular obedience comes because there is a slavery there. And regular obedience deepens and intensifies that slavery. We behave the way we do because we are the slaves of one master or another. Unconverted people are the slaves of one master or another. Everyone is the slave of something or someone.

The unconverted person is a slave of sin. Jesus said 'Whoever commits sin is a slave of sin' (John 8:34). The person who sins *does* what he *does*, because he *is* what he *is*. He is a slave in his being and nature; and so he or she behaves like a slave in obedience to his or her master. The person is a slave; and sin is the lord or master.

But the same thing is true of the Christian. When someone is converted he is radically changed. Conversion is not just saying a few words about believing in Jesus (although of course true faith has to be 'confessed'). True conversion is not just walking to the front of a meeting (although of course, public declaration that one is believing in Jesus is good and right). The important thing is that God has worked in the heart, God has opened the mind. God has touched our willingness to be committed to Jesus. When someone is truly converted, that person is being at that moment transferred from one master to another. And a change is taking place from an evil slavery (slavery to sin) to a happy slavery (slavery to obedience). The old person is ceasing to exist because 'I', I in my personality, am being united to Jesus Christ. True conversion is a radical new birth; it is transfer into a kingdom of grace. It is being ruled over by Jesus. So it is a transfer from one slavery to another, from the slavery of sin into the happy slavery to Jesus.

And just as slavery to sin leads to obedience to the master, so slavery to Jesus leads to obedience to the Master: 'you are the slaves of the one whom you obey'; in this case, slaves 'to obedience leading to righteousness'. There is something inevitable about it. Paul's point is obedience to righteousness is eventually virtually unavoidable. I do not want to exaggerate; and sin is certainly *possible* for the Christian. But we have died to Christ. We are new people. We are slaves to righteousness.

He goes on to describe their conversion, the event in their lives that made them 'happy slaves' to Jesus. *But thanks be to God that you were slaves of sin but you obeyed from the heart the form of teaching into which you were delivered* (Rom. 6:17). Do you realise what happened when you were converted to Jesus Christ? At the time of your conversion, you voluntarily obeyed the gospel. The gospel came to you with such power that it was like being poured into a mould. God acted in power.

This is Paul's description of what happens to us when God comes to us in the power of the Holy Spirit. The 'doctrine' or 'teaching' of the gospel about Jesus is coming to us with conviction. It is as though God takes hold of us and pours us into a specially shaped dish.

We obey from the heart. It is not just saying a few words or walking to the front in a meeting. That may be involved but it is more than that if there is true conversion. Our heart is being touched. We obey from the heart. Godliness is natural to us. We are slaves of righteousness!

This is why we obey the Lord Jesus Christ. It is because our conversion was a powerful thing. It changed us radically. It made us new people. Can we go on in sin, now that this grace of God has taken hold of us? No! How can we, if we have seen what has happened to us? It is only gross ignorance that ever mades a Christian think he can lightly sin.

Paul is answering the charge that grace encourages sin. But it is also an appeal to the Christian. We *are* slaves of righteousness. This is greatly encouraging. Righteousness has *enslaved* us, taken hold of us with great power. It is a mighty force in our lives. This is greatly encouraging. It tells us that we can live a godly life, and that there is a powerful reason for doing so. The grace of God is working where sin once abounded. We now are in a position to co-operate with what God has already done and follow through by putting our very bodies at His disposal.

18

THE POWER OF CONVERSION
(Romans 6:16–18)

True conversion is a powerful event. The Christian gets 'enslaved' to righteousness. Paul says, 'you are the slaves of the one whom you obey' (Rom. 6:16). Everybody is a slave of something or someone. The Christian is enslaved to Jesus. *But thanks be to God that you were slaves of sin but you obeyed from the heart the form of teaching into which you were delivered* (Rom. 6:17).

We know what it is like to cook some food in a pot in such a way that when the food comes out it is the same shape as the pot. People in Europe might make 'jelly'. They pour some sweet juice into a 'mould' and it sets firm and comes out with the same shape as the mould that it became hard in. In East Africa we often cook *ugali* or (as they call it further south) *nsima*. It is a maize meal that goes into the pot soft, but as it gets cooked it gets firm. When the housewife turns the maize-meal out on to a plate it has the same shape as the pot it was cooked in. If it goes into a square pot, it comes out square. If it goes into a small round pot, it comes out small and round. The 'mould' of the pot imposes its shape on it.

The gospel has a definite shape to it. It is like a mould, a specially shaped dish. It is the 'form'—the shape—of the teaching. By the Holy Spirit what we heard gets a grip upon us. We obey it. It is like being poured into a mould, a specially shaped pot. When we are saved, we come out 'cooked' in the right shape! Our conversion was a powerful thing. It changed us radically. It made us new people. It enslaved us. Can we go on in sin? No! How can we?

The Christian has been liberated. *But having been liberated from sin, you were enslaved to righteousness* (Rom. 6:18). The liberation he is speaking of must be understood in terms of what he has said earlier on and what he has been saying ever since chapter 5. He is not referring to total sinlessness, or total release from the flesh. But it means that our transfer to the kingdom of grace releases us from the kingdom or dominion of sin. Similarly being 'enslaved' to righteousness means that we have come into an entire realm of righteousness. God is ruling over us, and we have a new nature which powerfully leads us in the direction of righteousness. We have been enslaved by our being, taken captive into the kingdom of righteousness.

What is Paul doing in Romans 6:16–23?

(1) He is not contrasting the old life with the new life, in order that we may simply congratulate ourselves that we are in the one and not in the other. He is not saying, 'You have died to sin. Obedience is 100% inevitable. So all is well.' Although our being ruled over by grace is 100% certain, it does not mean that obedience is 100% inevitable. There would be no point in Romans 6:12–13 and in Romans 6:19b if total obedience were somehow 'forced' or irresistible and 100% inevitable. Transfer to the kingdom of grace has been done by God; putting the parts and faculties of our bodies at God's disposal has to be done by us.

(2) He is not hinting that they might not be saved, and then urging them to prove their salvation to themselves. His thought is *not* that godliness is inevitable for the Christian and therefore they are not truly saved if they do not live the godly life, and so they ought to start doubting straight away!

If he were doing that he would be evangelising the Roman Christians, seeking to get them 'really' saved. He would be saying, 'If you sin, you are not really saved.' If he were doing that it would be a subtle form of justification by works. He would be encouraging them to base assurance of salvation on works. But our works are never good enough to save us.

(3) He is not warning them against loss of salvation. The whole point is that righteousness has captured them and enslaved them.

What then is he doing in Romans 6:16–23? (1) *He is showing them the basis for their presenting their limbs and faculties to God*. The greatest thing has already been done. 'They'—in their true personalities—have died to sin. 'They' have been enslaved to righteousness. But Paul never says their bodies have been enslaved to righteousness. They must deal with that part of the matter themselves! They are kings and sovereigns, ruling and reigning with Christ. Well then, they must exercise their rule by not letting sin reign in their bodies. 'They' have been enslaved to righteousness, but sin rebels in their bodies. Although it is not possible for sin to reign in us, it is possible for it to reign in our bodies. But we are in control; we are under grace. So we must not let sin reign in our bodies.

(2) *He is appealing for consistency.* They must realise that they are slaves of righteousness and so follow through with practical self-presentation to God. There is indeed something that has been already achieved, this does not mean that godliness is automatic. It requires that we realise our position and 'follow through' with our practical self-presentation. He tells the Roman Christians that although they are slaves of righteousness by virtue of what God did for them at conversion, and by virtue of the way they responded to God at conversion, yet they must go on to work that out in presenting their bodily parts to God. It is absurd for anyone to continue in bondage in his actual *behaviour,* after he has gained his freedom in his *position* and in what has happened to him. He ought to make use of and work out the state of freedom which he has received. Although they made the right decision at conversion ('you obeyed!', verse 17), they must follow it through.

(3) There is a hint at the end of the chapter ('The wages of sin is death') that there will be serious consequences if they do not take him seriously. Sin cannot rule over us in our *position,* but sin can reign in our bodies and affect our *experience.*

19

YIELDING TO GOD
(Romans 6:19)

Paul explains that he is using an illustration. *I am speaking in a human way because of the weakness of your flesh.* Actually illustrations ought not to be necessary! We ought to be able to grasp the truth in itself without analogies. But we are so weak in spiritual things that we sometimes cannot grasp the truth without illustrations. Paul does not use many illustrations; he is not that type of person. There are plenty of stories in the Bible, but Paul reckons his readers have the Holy Spirit and are in a position to grasp the teaching as he puts it to them head-on. Nevertheless he sometimes uses illustrations like slavery and running a race. He uses the illustration of marriage and of grafting branches into a tree. So here he is using the analogy of slavery because he wants us to grasp hold of something. It is not a perfect illustration, so Paul explains why he has to use it. Slavery to Jesus is not the miserable, oppressive thing that slavery was for many in the ancient world. It is not something we want to run away from as Onesimus did. Slavery to Jesus is a happy slavery. His slavery is liberty. But although the illustration is not perfect, Paul wants to help us. It is because of your spiritual weakness, he says, that I have to use an illustration, but this will help you!

Now he asks them to 'follow through' with this happy slavery that God has given them. Once before Paul moved from what had happened to us ('Reckon yourself to have died . . .', Rom. 6:11) to what we should do ('Do not let sin reign . . . Yield your members', Rom. 6:12–13). Now he follows the same order again. He moves from what has happened to us ('Being made free from sin', Rom. 6:18) to what we should do, *For as you made the parts of your body available to be slaves in the service of impurity and of lawlessness leading to more lawlessness, so now make the parts of your body available to be slaves in the service of righteousness leading to growing sanctification.*

This is something we have to do ourselves. Our freedom from sin has been given to us. God has transferred us to the kingdom of His grace and we are slaves of righteousness. The yielding of the parts of our body and of our faculties is up to us. We do it. It is working out something that has already happened to us. We have already been put under God's grace. It is *because* we are under God's ruling grace that we are told to yield the constituent parts of our physical make-up.

This is the reverse of what we did in days gone by. In our unsaved days we would allow our physical frame to be used in the interests of sin. Our eyes and ears and hands and feet and tongue did things and went to places and said things that were entirely in the interests of sin. They led us into ever-increasing self-centredness and lawlessness. Now we are to do the exact opposite. We use every part of our bodies for God and for Jesus. Our voices are for God. The places we go and the literal things we do are to be for God. Our imaginations and intellect and abilities are all to be presented for the service of God and His kingdom.

The result is 'growing sanctification'. When you gave the bits and pieces of your life to the satisfying of sin, that sin grew. You were led into more and more lawlessness. Now, says the apostle, do the exact opposite. Before, your giving yourself to sin led to ever-increasing lawlessness. But if you will now present your limbs and faculties to God, it will lead to increasing godliness.

The word Paul uses ('growing sanctification') is parallel to but contrasts with his words 'lawlessness leading to more lawlessness'. It means not simply the condition of holiness but *growing* consecration. The result of our yielding our limbs and faculties to God will be that our lives will become increasingly God-centred.

This is the way to live! A life of yielding our limbs and faculties to God is a growing life. The path of the righteous will be a life that 'shines brighter and brighter until the full day' (Prov. 4:18). We make the parts of our body available as slaves in the service of righteousness. And this leads to growing sanctification.

The phrase 'in the service of righteousness' is not to be taken narrowly and individualistically. It does not refer only to prayer and fasting and self-denial and personal discipline. It is a life of growing positive purity. Old habits get broken. We treasure more and more the positive lessons the Lord Jesus Christ is teaching us. We grow in skill. We learn to watch our weak points where we find ourselves being taken aside into ways and habits that do not glorify God. Supremely we learn we have to watch our tongues. We learn how to grow in love. It includes a life of good relationships. It is mainly love! It has social aspects to it. Biblical holiness includes a concern for the needy, for structures of society, for the unborn child, for the use of wealth. It has things to say about marriage, about neighbourliness, about property, about the widow, the orphan, the immigrant. It is an entire kingdom of righteousness.

The exhortation is positive, not negative. It is encouraging, not threatening. The emphasis is on the privilege of serving God. We are positively to put ourselves at the disposal of God. The stress is on positively and actively promoting righteousness in our own lives and in the world in which we live.

20

LEARNING TO HATE SIN
(Romans 6:20–21a)

Paul has urged that the Christian cannot be complacent about sin (6:15) and he has gone on to explain why. Although everyone is a servant of something (6:16), in the case of the Christian his conversion was like being poured into a mould (6:17). He was released from the ruling power of sin (6:18). Paul is now asking that we should co-operate and develop what God has done for us by actually yielding the parts of our physical constitution to God.

He wants to motivate us even more. He wants us to reject our wicked past (6:20–21a) as an entirely useless and fruitless stage of our existence.

He reminds them of their past. *For when you were the slaves of sin, you were free in the matter of righteousness* (Rom. 6:20). It does not mean that they were all as bad as anyone can possibly be, and it does not mean that they were 'free' in the sense that God did not care what they did. But they were not slaves of righteousness, They did not care much about righteousness. They had no relationship to it whatsoever.

But Paul asks *What fruit then did you get at that time?* Did that kind of life ever do them any good? He answers: *Fruit of which you are now ashamed!*

If we see the godless life as a fruitless life, we shall view it with intense repulsion. Paul wants to produce in us something like the emotional reaction we have when we have been through a period of intense suffering. Some time ago I went through an experience that caused me the most intense distress. I happened to be in a village where a certain type of music was being played, and while I was there various things happened to me that caused great suffering for a while. I need not go into the details, but the point of my story is that for about a year after that experience, if ever I heard a piece of music vaguely resembling the music I heard at that time, I would shudder! Cold sweat would break out. I had a feeling of revulsion that I can scarcely put into words. A year went by before I could think about that situation without being in the grip of extreme disgust.

David had that kind of experience once. There was once a rebellion in his kingdom that caused David terrible suffering and led to the death of his son Absalom who had rebelled against him. Some years later there was a minor rebellion—a much smaller affair altogether. Amasa, David's military general at that period was rather casual about it and 'delayed and took longer than the time David had allocated to him' (2 Sam. 20:5). But David was aghast! 'Now this Sheba will do us more harm than Absalom did!' (2 Sam. 20:6). David had a violent emotional antagonism towards anything that reminded him of the hated days of suffering he had been through when Absalom rebelled. Whenever he was in any situation that reminded him of those days, he would react. 'Oh no! Not that! I don't want to be in anything like that again!' It was a violent emotional reaction to the days gone by that he now viewed with hatred.

So Paul is reminding them of their past. His hope is that they will view it with horror and seek to get as far away from the life of sin as they can get. *Don't you remember those days?* asks Paul. *They were days of slavery. Sin ruled over you. You were spiritually blind. You were alienated from God and blind to your own wickedness. What fruit came to you in those days? Fruit of which you are now ashamed! What good did sin do for your conscience? None at all. What real satisfaction did it give you? Where did it lead to in relationships with other people? Did it bring you damage or blessings?* They know the answer. As they look back they are filled with shame at the kind of things they did when they were without Christ.

We must react to sin in the way David reacted to Sheba. Oh no! Not that again! I do not want ever to take one step in the direction of anything like that! Think of the way the 'prodigal son' of Luke 15 must have viewed the days of his wanderings. How far he had been from his father! What a fool he was to ruin his life! How hungry he felt when everything went bad and his friends left him! How desperate he was to escape his predicament! How glad he was to get home!

Every Christian has the same memories. We remember times when we were so ignorant, so wayward. We recall the sheer uselessness of days without God. They brought nothing to us that was any good. How are we to view sin? Sin is an enemy.

It comes to us like a friend, wanting to pull us into the old paths we escaped from. Sin wants to get us back into the clutches of jealousy, animosity, bitterness of spirit, impurity, self-centredness. Paul wants us to view sin as a deadly enemy. We were slaves to it once. Now we are slaves to righteousness. But as we look back on our old enemy, it is like Absalom's rebellion all over again. We are aghast ever to find ourselves taking one step into those ways of sin. 'Never again!' we say. 'Never again!' I got nothing good from sin. It fills me with shame. I do not want to lose my peace of conscience. I do not want to grieve the Spirit. I do not want God to have to chastise me. That life of sin was only destroying me. I am not going to go anywhere near it. Never again!

21

THE ROAD TO RUIN
(Romans 6:21b–22)

We have asked ourselves the question, what exactly is Paul doing in Romans 6:16–23? The Christian has been liberated from sin. But Paul has more to say than just that. I have suggested that Paul is showing them the basis for their presenting their limbs and faculties to God. He is appealing for consistency, and is giving a hint that the way in which they live still does matter. They should, they may, they can, and they must yield their bodies as living sacrifices to God. Sin cannot rule over us in our *position*, but sin can reign in our bodies and affect our *experience*.

In verse 19 he asked them to 'make the parts of your body available to be slaves in the service of righteousness'. He is encouraging them and motivating them. They must learn to hate sin. 'What fruit did you get?' Nothing but that which brought them shame.

Now he seeks to persuade them in another way. What is the end of the two pathways, sin and righteousness? He is reminding them that that kind of life which they left was only leading them to death. It is not that he thinks they can ever die because of sin. He has already told them that they are 'in Christ' and that death can never rule over Christ. They are 'in Christ' and therefore death no longer has any dominion over them. But sin kills the person who is unsaved and a slave of sin. Christians must not dabble with the judgement that comes upon the unsaved.

'The end of those things is death.' When this death first came to Adam (Gen. 2:16) it involved a broken relationship with God, damaged relationships with people, a damaged relationship with the world, and a physical decay in himself that would terminate in physical death.

All of this, and more, continues in the children of Adam.

If these Roman Christians do not decisively get to hate sin, they will be hurt by death even though they do not come into its realm. Sin kills. It is not that Paul believes they can ever die spiritually in the full sense of the term. 'They'—in their true personality—have died to sin and have died to death!

He has denied that they can ever die and he will go on to do so in even more extreme terms in Romans chapter 8. But although 'they'—in their central personalities—cannot die, nevertheless it remains true the wages of sin is still death. They will reap death in their *experience* no matter what they may be in their position, if they do not respond to what he says. He is warning us that we can be slaves in our habits even though we are free in our position. He is speaking of unsaved people and the unsaved pre-conversion part of their lives when he says, 'Over those things you are now ashamed.' He immediately goes on to say *But now having been set free from sin and having been enslaved to God you have your fruit for sanctification and the end is eternal life* (Rom. 6:22). He says in effect, you were lined up for spiritual death, you were doing things that you are now ashamed of. But then something happened. God poured you into His 'mould' and righteousness took over as the king of your life. You never got any fruit before, but now you truly do have fruitfulness in your life. 'The fruit you get is sanctification', and the end of the road, the end of this life of enslavement to godliness that you are living, is eternal life.

It is a hint that if they walk along the pathway that leads to death, they are doing a most strange and weird thing. In such a case a slave to righteousness is walking along the pathway that belongs to slaves to death! A slave to righteousness is walking in one way, when grace is pushing him, pulling him, manipulating him, in an entirely different direction along an entirely different pathway. The sin of a Christian is greater rebellion than the sin of the unsaved! It invites great chastening, great rebuke. If these Roman Christians see what it would mean to play with sin and refuse to yield their limbs and faculties to God, they would shudder at the horrible thought of a Christian doing such an ignorant and bizarre thing as to walk along the pathway that leads to death.

Paul only barely hints at this possibility here, but he is rather more explicit later. 'If you live according to the flesh you are going to die' (Rom. 8:13). True, he uses in that place not the simple future sense ('You shall die') but a form of Greek which means something like 'you are intending—the way you are going—to die' or (we could paraphrase) 'you are following a route that will kill you'.

Here Paul is only barely hinting at this but he does have a reason for telling them what the route of sin leads to. They must not play around with sin. Although they are slaves to righteousness, sin kills. It may not send them to eternal hell—it will not—but it remains true that the wages of sin is death. That kind of life you used to lead, says Paul, is a life that now you are ashamed of. You know it is a life that leads to death. So keep off it altogether. God has done something for you that lifted you off that highway altogether, so don't be such a grotesque and weird phenomenon, a slave of righteousness walking along a highway belonging only to the slaves of death.

22

THE NEW LIFE
(Romans 6:22)

The end of the sinful life is death. But the Christian has been totally and radically removed from that pathway and put on to another route altogether. Paul says *But now having been set free from sin and having been enslaved to God, you have your fruit for sanctification and the end is eternal life.*

Much of what he says is simply repeating what he has put to us already.

(1) *The Christian has been set free from sin.* He has said something like this already. We have died to sin (6:2), what we used to be is dead and buried (6:3), our old self has gone (6:6–7). We have seen what this means. He is not teaching any kind of sinless perfectionism. He is not denying that the Christian has 'the flesh'. On the contrary he has said earlier that the 'body of sin' is still present, sin is still a problem that the Christian has to deal with. But the Christian has been 'set free from sin' in the sense of having been removed from being 'in Adam' and having been placed in Christ and therefore under the rule of grace. Sin does not rule over him.

(2) *The Christian has been enslaved to God.* This is a very powerful and strong word. It is a very great and mighty thing that has happened to the Christian. It is a great change, a complete change. He is utterly removed from the dominion of sin and put under the dominion of grace. God's grace has also taken up residence in his life and rules powerfully from within. It is not an ambition or something the apostle hopes will be true one day. It is already true; it has already happened. We have been poured into the mould of the gospel and are internally propelled towards righteousness (6:17); we are the servants of righteousness which governs and controls us (6:18). We are internally driven by God's ruling and reigning grace.

So sin is a nuisance to the Christian, sin attacks the Christian, but sin is not the king or ruler over the Christian.

When sin pushes the Christian into sin, it does so with deceit. Sin actually does not have the right or the authority to do this. The Christian is not in the realm of sin or Satan at all.   A Christian who sins is a Christian who has been listening to the counterfeit claims of the devil. Actually if the Christian resists the devil there is nothing the devil can do about it. The wicked one cannot touch us (1 John 5:18). We have already conquered the evil one (1 John 2:13–14). The world is in the grasp of the evil one (1 John 5:19) but we are not!

(3) So Paul says 'you have your fruit'. You have it; it is there already. The 'fruit' is the new position you are in, the new power working within you. This is something that is true of every Christian. If you are a Christian this is true of you already. No one is a Christian who has not been enslaved by right- eousness. It does not mean that we always feel this way, and it does not mean that violence is done to our responsibility. Nevertheless the life of having been placed in Christ is a life where something has happened. You are not the person you used to be. You have your fruit! You have been enslaved to God and God takes very seriously His ownership of us. That is the result of your changed position. You have it! As a result of being poured into God's mould and enslaved, it has produced something in you, a new nature, a new ability to present your bodies to God.

(4) *This fruit, consisting in new ability, is 'unto sanctification'.* It makes it possible for us to live a life of growing devotedness to God. You have been bought with a price. You are not your own. At the time of your conversion you may not have grasped hold of the full implications of what had happened to you. But realise it now! You had no fruit before, but you do have fruit now. The life of sin produced nothing good, but God will act powerfully within your life. You are owned by Him, just as any slave in the ancient world was owned by someone. Now God is going to be acting within you. You need to work out your salvation because God is at work within you to will and to work for His good pleasure.

The fruit you get is 'unto sanctification'. The fruit is not sanctification. The fruit is your new position, but it is 'unto sanctification'. It is a growing advancing progressing life you are in.

You have to have a position before you can grow in it. But when you have a certain position then you can grow in it.

The Christian *has* the fruit of being enslaved to sin. He is in grace. Now he can 'grow in grace' (2 Pet. 3:18), not grow *towards* grace, or grow to *get* grace, but grow *in* grace. The Christian can grow in obedience, in graciousness, in endurance and patience, in fearlessness, in prayerfulness, in his inventiveness for finding new ways of serving God, in love. He has his fruit, the power of righteousness working within him. But it is 'for progressing in holiness', 'for sanctification'.

(5) The further end of sanctification is reaping 'eternal life', harvesting life and energy from God Himself. 'Eternal life' is the energy and life of God in our lives. It is the conscious enjoyment of life flowing from God. It is ever-flowing animation in the things of God. It is consciously enjoying freedom from sin. It is boldness to take hold of God's will for our lives. It is liveliness from God which starts now and lasts for ever.

23

THE WAGES OF SIN
(Romans 6:23)

The Christian has definitely and conclusively been placed upon the road that leads to life. He has been powerfully 'enslaved' to righteousness.

Paul is reminding the Christian of these two ways because he wants them to 'follow through' on what has happened to them. He wants them to yield their bodies to God. There is also the possibility that they might be so foolish as to try to walk on the wrong road! From what he has said one might think that was hardly possible. The Christian is 'enslaved' to righteousness. Yet it is possible to sow to the flesh and 'reap corruption' (Gal. 6:8), so Paul's mentioning the way of death is not an idle matter. Their position has changed forever. They are slaves of righteousness. But let them not take one step on a road which destroys and corrupts. Otherwise, whether they are slaves of righteousness or not, their *experience* will be that they will corrupt themselves and destroy themselves and be 'saved through fire'. They are on the right road, but let them not dabble with the wrong one. *For the wages of sin is death . . .*

God warned the human race that 'death' would follow sin. Adam did not heed the warning and 'death' followed. He lost his happiness in fellowshipping with God. He was excluded from God's presence. His relationship with his wife was soured. Murder and violence came into the human race. Creation itself fell and became twisted and spoiled. Physical decay set in. Adam began to move toward physical death from the second he sinned. The race became vulnerable to evil powers (which is the point of Genesis 6:1–8), and the day came when God had to almost wipe out the human race (in the flood), and start again with new restraints and boundaries for the human race after Noah.

Sin gets paid its wages. 'Death' comes into our experience when we sin. But there is also the final and eternal consequence of sin in an ultimate and final death. If there is 'life after death' for the child of God, there is 'death after death' for the wicked.

This final death is love withdrawn. God's love is righteous love. He loves righteousness (Ps. 11:7), and He loves righteous people (Ps. 146:8). Even when He loves the fallen sinful race it is with a view to bringing the sinner to be righteous, first with a righteousness 'reckoned' his, and then with a righteousness worked into his life.

It is possible for God's love to be withdrawn. God's love for his people is 'everlasting love' (Jer. 31:3). But the wickedness of the unsaved who are walking on the road to destruction will eventually result in love withdrawn. 'Because of the wickedness . . . I will love them no more' (Hos. 9:15). While the unsaved person is alive he is loved. His very being alive is the proof of God's continued love. Grace is still on offer. The love of God is still being held out. But the wages of sin is death. And there is a 'death beyond death'; it is when the offer of the experience of God's love is withdrawn.

This final death is the experience of just payment. It is retribution. This is why it is called 'wages'. A wage is something that is earned. Heaven is not a 'wage', but final death beyond death is the payment of salary for what has been worked for. It is justice. God currently offers 'free gift', but if 'free gift' is not accepted, what is received instead is 'wages'. God currently is offering mercy, but if mercy is not received what is finally given is justice.

This final death is anguish. It is regret; it is exclusion. It is being left in outer darkness. It is being outside the banquet-hall, outside the wedding feast. It is facing the shut door. It is the experience of being ignored. It is being abandoned. It is frustration, remorse, the wringing of the hands, the gnashing of the teeth. It is staying with one's unchanging sinful character. It is humiliation, public disgrace. It is loneliness and isolation. It is everyone knowing you were wrong. It is contempt, shame.

It is lost opportunity. It is the day when repentance no longer avails and faith is no longer possible because everything is seen and proved. It is bowing the knee when it is too late, it is confessing that Jesus is Lord when it is too late for that confession to bring you any personal blessing. It is when, after Jesus has endured your saying, 'We will not have this man to reign over us', He gives you your request and you hear Jesus say to you, 'You depart from me'. No one will have any complaints. Everyone will know justice has been done. Death, the wages of sin, is God-less-ness in this life. It is physical termination without God, and then death beyond death for ever.

Praise God, a Christian has been delivered from this road! What a relief, what deliverance! The Christian is the slave of righteousness! God has stepped into his life, taken hold of him, poured him or her into the mould of Jesus. Can a Christian ever experience anything of this death? Ultimately, the answer is no! But he can go *through* it. He can be saved 'through' God's fire (1 Cor. 3:15). It is a mysterious subject and I scarcely know enough about it. But he that overcomes shall not be 'hurt by' the second death (Rev. 3:9). On account of fornication, covetousness and idolatry 'the wrath of God is coming *upon the children of disobedience*' (Eph. 5:6). You are *not* one of them, but 'be not partakers with them'. You *are* children of the light. Take care to walk as children of the light.

24

ETERNAL LIFE
(Romans 6:23b)

The wages of sin is death, *but the free gift of God is eternal life in Christ Jesus our Lord.* God is giving us the gift of life but it is *progressively and continually* given over to us. It is like what happens when we provide for our children. We are going to minister to our own earthly children all that they need. We shall clothe them, feed them, guide them, provide for them. But this provision is not given all at once and in one gigantic lump.

It is the same with God and His children. The very second we believe in Jesus we have eternal life. But this eternal life is to be administered to us. It goes on and on.

It is a gift, a sheer wonderful unselfish kind compassionate gift from the God of mercy and grace and goodness. If sin gets paid a wage, holiness does *not* get a 'wage'. God rewards our godliness, and yet even the reward is never in any way 'earned'. The reward itself is sheer gift, sheer mercy. God Himself is the one who has been working in us. How can He reward us when He is the one who was willing and working for His good pleasure? But God loves to reward us, even when He was the one who enabled us to lay hold of His blessing in the first place. As we live the life of holiness we lay hold of the 'free gift' and His life flows into us.

This is the point of Romans 6:23. We reap eternal life by sowing to the Spirit (Gal. 6:8). We have to 'lay hold' of eternal life (1 Tim. 6:12). The end-product of yielding ourselves to God is that we enter into the actual experience of eternal life (Rom. 6:22). The grace of God reigns in us so that we are experiencing eternal life (Rom. 5:21); we are alive unto God (6:11); we are able to lay hold of eternal life in our actual experience.

What is eternal life? The phrase comes 44 times in the New Testament (I am about to mention all of them). Eternal life is Jesus Himself! The apostle John, at the beginning of his first letter, says Jesus is the 'eternal life' which was with the Father

(1 John 1:2). At the very end of the letter he says it again: 'This One is the true God and eternal life' (1 John 5:20). Eternal life is essentially a regular day-by-day everlasting knowledge of Jesus (John 17:2, 3). It is spiritual knowledge, fellowship-knowledge, the knowledge of a Person, it is the enjoyment of God's Presence. It is tasting and seeing that God is good (Ps. 34). It is the experience of God's lovingkindness comforting and strengthening us (Ps. 119:76, 82). It is when our heart burns within us (Luke 24).

It will help us if we look at it from three angles, as the New Testament does.

Sometimes the stress is on what I could call *initial salvation*. When John's Gospel speaks of 'eternal life' the emphasis is occasionally on the 'first step', the faith that delivers us from being on the road to destruction and brings us into life (John 3:15, 16, 36; 10:28). The Jewish leaders thought they had eternal life merely by possessing the Scriptures (John 5:39) but Jesus tells them they need to take that initial step of coming to Him in order that they might get that life (John 5:40). In John 4:36 Jesus is one reaping the harvest. Many Samaritans are on their way to coming to Him. So He is reaping a harvest 'into eternal life'. A similar emphasis on the first beginning of eternal life is found also in Acts 13:46, 48 and 1 Timothy 1:16.

But generally speaking the New Testament emphasis is not on the first step of the Christian life. It concentrates more on the *daily experience* of having and progressively entering into a life that comes from God. Even in John's Gospel 'eternal life' is not a momentary thing that happens to us when we are first saved. It is something that we 'have' from the moment we first believe (John 3:36; 5:24). Jesus' living water goes on 'springing up into eternal life' (John 4:14). John chapter 6 is about labouring (6:27) to get the bread of life. It is not simply a momentary once-for-ever thing that Jesus has in mind. Truly, it has a starting point, but it goes on for the rest of one's life. Jesus is the bread of life (John 6:47–48). We feed on Him daily as the Israelites fed daily on the manna. In so doing we get 'life'; we come 'alive' with a liveliness towards God. It goes on to the resurrection (John 6:40, 54) and is daily experienced by heeding the words of Jesus (6:68). In John 12 'eternal life' is experienced by the on-going process of not loving one's life (John 12:25). The words which Jesus speaks at the Father's command are a perpetual source of life to those who receive them (John 12:20). It is this 'eternal life' which is experienced when we live for God. Romans chapter 6 has been telling us of the basis of our living for God.   Can we go on in sin so that grace may abound? No, not at all! We have died to the entire realm and rule of sin. We have been enslaved unto righteousness. We have the fruit of that immediately. We are alive unto God, we have new abilities, new power. We are able to grow in the grace of God in which we are standing. But the *end product* is to experience a richer and fuller flowing in our lives of 'eternal life'. It begins in this life. Even here and now we are conscious of God. Those who sow to the Spirit reap back from the Spirit the energy and joy that comes from knowing that we are pleasing God. The life of God burns within us.

25

LAYING HOLD OF ETERNAL LIFE
(Romans 6:23b)

The wages of sin is death, *but the free gift of God is eternal life in Christ Jesus our Lord*. The end product and goal of our living for God is the experience of eternal life.

This is a common theme of Scripture. When Titus 1:2 talks about the 'knowledge of the truth which is according to godliness', he adds 'in hope of eternal life'. The eternal life is something reaped as the result of godliness. In Titus 3:7 justification is one step along the road to inheritance, and the inheritance is 'according to the hope of eternal life'. Once again 'eternal life' is something reaped and inherited.

Eternal life is the heart of everything that God wants to give us in and through Jesus. It is the entire spread of the blessings of God. They can all be summarised in one word: life. God wants us to be truly alive. God wants us to be lively people with the liveliness that comes not from temperament or physical health but with the liveliness that comes from God. We are alive unto God!

The rich young ruler asked about 'eternal life' (Matt. 19:16). He was asking more than how to be saved. He was asking about 'inheriting' (Matt. 19:19; Mark 10:17; Luke 18:18) eternal life. The answer he was given was: get to a level of holiness that outstrips the Mosaic law, attend to the personal requirements of Jesus and get involved in Jesus' ministry team. The lawyer of Luke 10:25 was also asking about 'inheriting eternal life' (Luke 10:25); he summarised the thrust of the law in terms of getting to love God and all people everywhere (Luke 10:26–27) and was told that this was all that he had to do to 'live' (Luke 10:28).

This is what God wants, to administer life to us on a daily basis. We basically have it if we know Jesus (1 John 5:11). But there is more. We are to have life *and* have it more abundantly

(John 10:10). 'This is the promise . . . eternal life' (1 John 2:25). We shall not be experiencing it if we are 'murdering our brother' (1 John 3:15).   The pleas in 1 John that we should hold to faith in Jesus as the Son of God come in the flesh, and walk in the light, and live a life of love, are written—says 1 John 5:13—in order that you might know in experience that you have eternal life.

There is a third aspect to this matter. We are sometimes told that the last phrase of 'eternal life' is given to us when Jesus comes the second time. Then the righteous 'go away' into eternal life (Matt. 25:46). They have the last phase of eternal life in 'the age to come' (Mark 10:30; Luke 18:30). We are to live in such a way that we get rich blessings on this day when we get honour and immortality and 'eternal life' (Rom. 2:7). We have to lay hold of eternal life (1 Tim. 6:12) and this is not just by our first believing. It comes by 'laying up in store for themselves a good foundation' (1 Tim. 6:19). These Scriptures are speaking of what will happen in judgement day. This will help us to understand Romans 6:23. The end product of godly living is to *experience* the life of God in this world. We are in Christ. We have died to sin. But there are still two routes we can follow. We can still corrupt the life that has been given to us. We can still reap corruption. No doubt our position is eternally secure in the sense that our justification shall never be lost. Those whom God has justified He has glorified. It is as good as done. But this is not all that can be said. There are *still* two roads before us. We can reap corruption. Our position cannot be lost but it can be corrupted (Gal. 6:8), our life can wither and die (Rom. 8:13). We shall not go to hell but we can lose a great deal and experience what it is to taste the wrath of God. Mortification of the deeds of the body are necessary if we are to have this life in *experience*. We have it by *position in God's kingdom* but more is to be done if we are to have it in experience.   Paul holds out the hope of eternal liveliness! This is the gift of God, he says. This is what God wants to give you. It is a present experience.   It means enjoying this life because God is present with you. It is conscious fellowship with God. It is enjoying His good gifts as blessings which come from His hands. It is daily awareness of Jesus. It is finding liveliness towards Him springing up in our hearts. It is the propellant that we experience when Jesus speaks to us, the energy and nourishment that we feel within ourselves when we are rejoicing in the Lord, the vim and vigour of being at peace with God, being animated. The drive, the enthusiasm, the sparkle that comes from God Himself. I do not refer to animal spirits or extrovert temperament. The gloomiest of temperaments can experience 'eternal life'. It comes with a clear conscience. It comes initially when we first believe on Jesus. It flows 'more abundantly' by yielding our bodies to God as living sacrifices. It is administered to us on a daily basis: 'the free gift of God is eternal life'.

Who can say what the final phase of this eternal life will be? It does not yet appear what we shall be. But we shall be more alive than we have ever been. The eternal life of Jesus will flow within us. We can scarcely say what it will be like. It will be joy. It will be shining like the sun with radiant holiness. It will be vibrant energy. The end of our life for God will be that we shall be alive with the life of God as never before. The life lived for God now will lead on into 'eternal life in Christ Jesus our Lord'.

PART TWO

Romans 7:1–25

26

THE QUEST FOR GODLINESS
(Romans 7:1–25)

Romans chapter 7 is the most controversial chapter of Romans. It is not the most important (perhaps 5:12–21 or the end of chapter 3 has that honour). It is not the most beautiful and exciting (Romans chapter 8 has that distinction). Chapter 11 is perhaps the most amazing (as Paul's expression of wonder and worship suggests in 11:33–36). Chapter 12 is perhaps the most practical. Chapter 1:18–32 is the most horrific. Chapter 9 has aroused the *deepest* controversy, but the end of Romans chapter 7 has provoked the *widest* controversy, in the sense that the range of opinions has been very varied.

The key question is: how does the Christian get power and resources for his life? How does Paul want us to live? So far in the letter to the Romans, he has said that God wants us to live by persistent faith in Jesus. This was the theme of the end of Romans chapter 4. God wants us to 'inherit' the promises that God has made to us. We do this not by law but by persisting in faith. We are not to stagger at what God has said but by persisting in faith we shall lay hold of everything He wants to do to us and through us.

God wants us to live directly under His grace. Romans 5 told us that whereas we were ruled by sin, we are now ruled by God's grace. In chapter 6 of Romans Paul told us we have died to sin and must present the various parts of our bodies to God. At this point we might be asking the question, 'Does Paul have any guidelines to Christian conduct?' He has not mentioned any 'rules' so far. Could the law given to Israel be the guideline? That would include the various regulations about circumcision, about holy days, about clean and unclean foods. Or could it be that we are simply under the 32 verses that give to us (twice over) the 'Ten Commandments'. That would involve keeping Saturday as a holy day. Actually, Paul has not given the slightest hint of anything like that. He has said that the law was given only to Israel and that others are without the law (2:12), that it gives knowledge only of sin (3:20), that it produces wrath (4:15) and increases the power of sin (5:20), and that we are not under it (6:14).

What guideline then are we under? Paul has not given us much of an answer so far in the letter to the Romans. We would gather (if we read no further than the first six chapters) that somehow we are simply meant to know God's will. Later on he will talk about being led by the Holy Spirit. He will finally get to giving us exhortations himself (chs. 12—15). In the middle of that section (13:8–10) he will tell us to focus on love and say that love leads us into the fulfilment of the whole law of Moses. Paul's main point in Romans chapter 7 is to tell us that we should not try to live under the Mosaic law. We actually have 'died' to it, in order to be fruitful towards God.

The main point of Romans chapter 7, then, is that we are free from the law of Moses and that we live in the power of the Holy Spirit. We have died to the Mosaic law, and any similar law. (The 'law of Christ' is a different kind of law altogether.) The Christian is released from being 'in Adam' (5:12–21), released from death, from judgement, from sin. More surprisingly he is released from the Mosaic law. I say 'more surprisingly' because who would have guessed that Paul would put the holy law of God in the company of sin and death and judgement as something we are to be released from? But that is precisely what Paul does. He uses the same language concerning the law ('you have died to the law') as he had used of sin ('you have died to sin')!

When we inspect the whole chapter we can see that it breaks down into sections.

In Romans 7:1–4 he makes a basic statement. We have died to the law in order to be fruitful towards God. The argument goes like this. Any law rules over that person only while he is alive. The law can never die, but we can and do die to the law through Jesus. This is precisely what happened. We have died to the law.

In Romans 7:5–6, which I believe to be very important verses and the key to everything he says, he compares what it is like to be 'in the flesh' and 'under the law' (on the one side) with being 'in the Spirit' (on the other side). The result of being under law (verse 5) is agony and spiritual death. I am suggesting that verse 5 is the key to the rest of the chapter. In verse 6 he puts the other side of the comparison and tells us what it is like to be in the Spirit and 'married' to Jesus.

Romans 7:7–12 takes up the question 'Is the law a sinful thing in itself?' His answer is 'No', but he says if we ever come under the command not to covet we shall discover that it gives an intense experience of what sin is like.

Romans 7:13–25 takes up the question again, and in a deeper way describes what it is like to be under the law. The 'wretched man' of Romans 7:13–25 is a description of the maximum the holy law of God can do in the unconverted person. It is an exposition of verse 5.

So the thrust of the whole chapter is to get us to abandon for ever the attempt to live 'under' law. We come at godliness in a different way. We are, of course, concerned about righteousness. But we get there by faith, by fellowship with Jesus, by walking in the Spirit. If we walk in the Spirit deliberately, we fulfil the law of God accidentally. We do not need to be 'under' it. Godliness comes indirectly by faith, by Jesus, by the Spirit. The law cannot produce the righteousness we want. A direct relationship with Jesus can.

27

DEATH RELEASES FROM LAW
(Romans 7:1–4)

If you do not live under Jesus, what do you live under?
The answer is you live depending on your own understanding,
or upon tradition, or upon what you do or do not feel guilty
about, or you live according to the pressure that other people put
on you. Or you live on some kind of law. Maybe you are very
concerned to live according to God's law. Or you have a version
of what you think is God's law, for no one really keeps the Jewish
law. I have quite a few books on the Ten Commandments, which
all think they are expounding 'God's law'. However they all
focus on the Ten Commandments but rather ignore Exodus
20:22—23:33, Leviticus 18—20 and Deuteronomy 12—25 which
are the real and original expositions of the Ten Commandments.

But we are not to live under any of these things. We are
to live depending directly upon Jesus. We are to live under the
pressure of love, and say, 'The love of Christ constrains me.' We
are to live in fellowship with Jesus and His Spirit. We fulfil the
law indirectly, not by being directly under it.

Paul wants us to know that we have died to the law. He
starts to put it to us like this. *Do you not know, brothers and
sisters—for I am speaking to people who know the law—that the law
has authority over a man only as long as he lives* (Rom. 7:1)?

He starts with this basic principle. He is writing to
people who are very familiar with the law of Moses. Many of
them were Jews, as is clear from the way Paul answers so many
Jewish questions in this letter. Even the Gentiles in Rome seem
to have been influenced by the Jewish Christians. Those who
esteemed one day as more than another (Rom. 14:5) were
probably Christians influenced by the regulations concerning
various days that were kept as holy days according to the law.
Certainly they knew the Mosaic law well, and they would have
been very familiar with the Roman law as well, since they were
living in Rome, the capital of the empire.

So Paul says, 'I am speaking to people who know the law.' There is one thing that would be obvious to them. The law only operates when the person concerned is alive. Imagine someone commits a crime, and the legal authorities are wanting him for prosecution and possible imprisonment. But then the police or magistrates discover that that person has died. At that point they drop all concern about trying the criminal with any charges. The police no longer bother with him. The magistrates are no longer interested in summoning the man to court. The law only has authority over the person while he is alive.

Then in verses 2–3 he puts forward something that is both an example and an illustration at the same time. He says, *For a married woman is bound by law to her husband as long as he is alive, but if her husband dies, she is released from the law of marriage.* In this verse, an incidental point of interest is this. The relationship between verse 1 and verse 2 is the proof that when Paul uses the word 'man', he does not mean 'male', he means member of the human race. To say 'The law has authority over a male as long as he lives . . . for example a woman . . . ' does not make sense! The word often translated 'man' in verse 1 often has the sense of 'a person'. So we could translate, 'The law has authority over a human being as long as he or she lives . . . For example a woman . . . '.

Verses 2 and 3 are an illustration of what he said in verse 1. If in a marriage the man dies, his death means that no law about loyalty to him has any force. A death ends the legal obligation.

Verse 3 explains further. *So then, if she marries another man while her husband is still alive, she is called an adulteress. But if her husband dies, she is released from that law and is not an adulteress, even though she marries another man.* Marriage is lifelong. Paul is not discussing the possibility of divorce. It is only an illustration and he does not bring in complicating factors. If the woman marries during the lifetime of the husband she has done something illegal. The law is operating while the people concerned are alive. However, if a death takes place the situation is entirely changed. She is entirely released from the law that was binding her. She is entirely free to remarry. It would have been illegal before. Now she is free. The law that was restricting her is entirely irrelevant. A death puts the wife into an entirely different status. She is free to enter into another relationship without being troubled at all by the law which once bound her.

So it means that a person may come to be entirely free from a law, without that law being in any way ignored, without the authority of the law being reduced. A death may change the relationship to the law even though the law still exists.

All this is preparing for what Paul says in Romans 7:4. *So, my brothers, you also were made to die to the law . . . that you might belong to another . . .* The law of God cannot die. But the Christian has died! He has died in Christ as Paul explained so thoroughly in Romans chapter 6. This leaves the Christian free to pursue an entirely different kind of relationship. This is the heart of the matter. If you want to live a truly godly life, do not cultivate a relationship with the Mosaic law, cultivate a relationship directly with Jesus.

28

WHO IS UNDER THE LAW?
(Romans 7:4)

The point that Paul makes in verses 2 and 3 is an *example* of what he said in verse 1. Laws do not apply after death. Marriage is an example. In verse 4 he now uses the same idea of marriage as an *illustration*. It is a slight twist of thought. Now in verse 4 the woman stands for the believer; the first husband stands for the law; the second husband stands for Jesus.

It is a slightly awkward illustration because the law does not die. It is not the death of our husband (the law) that releases us. Rather we get released by the fact that we ourselves have died to the law. So the illustration is back-to-front. Yet Paul uses it because it brings out very clearly the way we may be in one relationship, then a death ends the relationship, and then there is the possibility of another relationship.

Romans 7:4 says that every Christian has died to the Mosaic law! It does not precisely mean that every Christian had been under the law for this is not strictly true. We were threatened by it. We know about it because of the fact that the Christian church arises out of Israel and 'the law' is in our Bible and points to Jesus. But it is not true that all unconverted people are under the Mosaic law.

In Rome some were under the law as a fact of history (the Jews). Some had been 'under the law', in the sense of having been intimidated by it, and living in fear and guilt and timidity. Some thought that because the law was for Israel and they had joined God's true believing Israel, maybe the law was for them. Everyone is in danger of coming under the Mosaic law in one way or another. But when God redeemed Israel from the law, He redeemed every believer from even the threat of it.

Romans 2:14 has sometimes been understood, wrongly, to teach that people are under the law without having the law. But that contradicts the language of the entire Bible. 'The law' is the system given to Moses. Gentiles do not have it. Romans 2 is

partly hypothetical but has Gentile Christians in mind who fulfil
the law by walking in the Spirit. Notice also the translation of
Romans 2:14, 'For whenever the nations, who do not have the
law by nature, do the things of the law', *not* 'For whenever
nations who do not have the law, by nature do the things of the
law . . .'. No one keeps the things of the Mosaic law 'by nature'
(including having a Jewish king, Deut. 17:15!) But 'the nations'
do not 'by nature' have Israel's law. 'By nature' in Romans 2:14
means 'by birth' (as in Ephesians 2:3 and Galatians 2:15).

Gentiles relate to God through conscience but the words
'the law' are not used in connection with conscience. In the
entire Bible Gentiles are notorious for not having the law. This is
the whole point of Romans 5:14; people before the law died
without transgressing any codified 'law'.

Gentiles were never given the law in the first place, and
Paul consistently and regularly describes Gentiles as people who
were without the law. When Paul uses the word 'law' he
normally is referring to the entire legal arrangements God gave
to Israel, and to Israel alone, at the time of Moses. Romans 9:4
speaks of the giving of the law as one of the special privileges of
Israel. So the idea that the entire world was given the law is
entirely wrong. The ten commandments themselves begin, 'I am
the LORD your God who brought you out of the land of Egypt,'
and this was true of Israel alone.

When salvation came, Jewish believers were redeemed
from the law, and *at the same time Jesus redeemed anyone else who
believed from ever having to come under the law.* In Galatians, Paul
spoke at one stage of 'we, who are Jews by nature' (Gal. 2:16). A
few lines later he is still using 'we' in this way, meaning 'we
Jews'. He says 'Christ redeemed *us* (us Jews) from the curse of
the law . . . in order that the promise of Abraham might come to
Gentiles' (Gal. 3:13, 14). While the law was there the Jew could
not have liberty and the Gentile could not come into 'Israel', the
people of God. 'Before faith came (we Jews) were kept in
custody under the law . . . Now that faith has come *we* (we Jews)
are no longer under a guardian. For *you* are *all* sons of God . . .
There is neither Jew nor Greek . . . If you belong to Christ, then
you are Abraham's seed' (Gal. 3:23–29). The whole argument
hinges upon the fact that the law was for Israel alone. Gentiles
could come under it only by being associated with Israel. When
Jesus died, believing Jews were released from being under the
law, *and therefore the threat to Gentiles was lifted at the same time.*

Jews and Gentiles were two groups with the law as the mark of distinction between the two (see Eph. 2:14). Jesus abolished the law and so made it possible for the two groups, Jews and Gentiles, to become one body by believing in Christ (Eph. 2:15-19).

This is the way Scripture presents the coming of the Saviour. It is set out in great detail in Isaiah. In the book of Isaiah the Servant of God comes to redeem Israel, but by redeeming Israel the world is redeemed as a side-effect. The coming of the Servant of God to Israel is the answer to the world's plight. Israel was meant to be a light to lighten the Gentiles, but failed miserably. The suffering Servant has to actually *be* Israel (the Messiah's name in Isaiah 49:3). The nations ('O islands . . . you peoples from afar') are invited to see a suffering Servant redeem His people, and so redeem them (Isa. 49:1-3).

So Romans 7:4 says that every Christian has died to the Mosaic law! The Gentiles were never under it. They can join God's true Israel without coming under the law. Christ died to the law and since we are in Christ those of us who are Gentile believers have died to the Mosaic law also.

29

YOU DIED TO THE LAW
(Romans 7:4)

The Christians in Rome have died to the law. *So, my brothers, you also were made to die to the law through the body of Christ . . .* It is a very radical statement. There are a number of principles involved, which we shall examine in the next few chapters.

Firstly, the Christians at Rome were married to the law. This is only an illustration and it must not be pressed too far. There are many ways in which the Christians could be under the law. Jews would be 'under the law' as a sheer fact of their history. Gentiles would be highly attracted to the law as a possible way of holiness. There would probably be some Christians around who were somewhat legalistic. There would be others who, when false teachers came saying, 'You must keep the law', would find their appeal tempting. In addition we know that some Christians at Rome were 'weak'; they were fussy about what meat they could eat and whether they had to keep holy days. Romans 15:7–13 makes one realise that the Mosaic law had something to do with these conflicts.

There are many Christians who are 'under the law'. They may not be well-informed about the Mosaic law, but many Christians try to 'live up to God's standards' and feel condemned by failure. Or they have a list of things that they feel God requires of them if they are to be spiritual. They may be severe with their bodies, they may fast too much and sleep too little, and feel very guilty eating a meal. Or they find it hard to enjoy God's world. Or they have strict regulations about clothing or meetings or ways of praying. They can have quite peculiar rules. They may be strictly against cinema but watch TV for hours! Or they have rules about who they can talk to or be seen with.

But all this is a wrong way of approaching godliness altogether! God's law is not the way of holiness. Being under our own feeble laws is even more useless. The way of holiness is to be under a Person, Jesus Himself!

For one reason or another the Roman Christians clearly had a problem, and were in effect 'married' to the law.

A second principle is: *all Christians have died to the law.* The law has many aspects. The Christian has died to all of them! The law has a *restraining* aspect. It held back sin because it threatened serious punishment. There were many crimes which were subject to the death penalty (adultery, delinquency in young people, dishonouring parents, giving out false prophecy, profaning the Saturday rest-day, and others). But the Christian has died to this way of being restrained from sin. His 'fear of the Lord' is different. It is fear of lost fellowship, fear of grieving the Spirit, fear of God's withdrawal.

The law had *a punishing aspect.* I have mentioned capital punishment, and there were other forms of restitution the law demanded. But the Christian is not under this legislation.

There is a *ritual aspect* to the law. There were various ceremonies the Jew had to go through. Think of the ritual in Numbers 5 which required a wife suspected of unfaithfulness to go through a ritual ordeal. The Christian has died to it all.

There was a *sacrificial* aspect to the law. Think of the five types of animal sacrifice.

There was a *calendrical* aspect of the law. Think of the three major festivals which required attendance at Jerusalem.

There were *national aspects* to the law. Think of the requirement that the leader of the nation be a Jew, and that Gentiles were not allowed inside the tabernacle.

There were *tribal aspects* to the law. Think of the requirement that the civic leader be of the tribe of Judah and the religious leader be of the tribe of Levi.

There were *economic aspects* to the law. Think of the requirements about the jubilee year. And think of the legislation about tithing. Also, there were *agricultural aspects* to the law.

Most people forget all of this when they think of the law. They tend to think only of the spiritual demands they think are in the law, and the punishment that the law demands.

The most difficult aspect of this matter is that the Christian has died to the moral and ethical aspects of the law. This sometimes troubles Christians because it sounds like licence to sin. But the moral demands of the law are abrogated because they are too low a level for Christian spirituality. Of course the basic demands of eight of the ten commands are met (we shall leave aside the questions that arise about the Sabbath; and the tenth command is in a category all of its own). Even the ten commandments are too low a level for Christian spirituality.

The truth is that Christian spirituality does not come through relating to a law. Spirituality comes through relating to a person, Jesus Himself. Accept the blood of Jesus for your salvation. Accept Jesus as your righteousness. Accept Jesus as your holiness. Accept Jesus as the one who will bring you to final glory. And now start fellowshipping with Jesus. Every day spend time with Him. You can read the law. But when you read it, don't say to yourself, 'How can I obey this?' Instead talk to Jesus. Say to Him, 'Lord how do you want me to go beyond all of this, that I am reading about in the law of Moses?' Jesus will answer you. The New Testament will confirm that what you think is the leading of the Spirit really *is* the leading of the Spirit, and you will be led by Jesus into ways of holiness. And you will go beyond the law!

30

A FRAGMENT OF HISTORY
(Romans 7:4)

Before we continue to unpack the principles in this radical statement, it would be helpful to look at a difficulty that has sometimes been caused by this 'dying to the law'. It has sometimes caused difficulty, because in the story of the church there has been a tendency to drift into moralism. When Paul spoke about 'the law' he was talking about everything that came down to us through Moses. He said that we have died to the entire Mosaic system. It is not a way of justification, nor is it a way of sanctification.

This doctrine of freedom from the Mosaic law and life under the grace of God was soon forgotten. One does not have to go very far into the story of the church before you find little grasp of the grace of God in Jesus. Within a century the church became full of moralism, more than full of grace. The great Augustine had a grasp of the grace of God but even he never quite went back to the apostle Paul with regard to the teaching about 'the law'.

In the thirteenth century a theologian named Thomas Aquinas was powerfully influential and wrote *Summa Theologiae* (A Summary of Theology), which includes many pages on 'The Old Law', the law of God given on Sinai. Thomas Aquinas formulated a doctrine of law using as a framework the thought of the Greek philosopher Aristotle, plus Paul and Augustine.

He divided the law into three. The *moral* laws are the basic principles of right and wrong. For Aquinas they are the same as 'natural law', the basic law on every one's conscience which can be deduced by unaided reason without the need of God's word. The *ceremonial* laws are the Old Testament legislation about sacrifices and holy days and so on. Aquinas thinks this part of the law is abolished, and is 'not only dead, but also deadly'. Then there are the *judicial* laws which are regulations concerning justice which were special to the nation of

Israel. He taught that judicial laws were abolished and are 'dead since they have no binding force but not deadly', and that if a ruler imposed them he was not guilty of sin.

Thomas Aquinas, like all theologians between Paul and Luther, taught that we are 'justified' before God by the good works of the new nature God's grace works in us. The law helps to guide our good works and (said Aquinas) the 'Old Law' of Moses has permanent value to guide us in righteousness even though parts of it have been abolished. Thomas Aquinas had no idea of Paul's teaching that Christ's righteousness is 'reckoned' ours when we believe in Jesus. His teaching became the basis of Roman Catholic doctrine.

At the time of the Reformation in the sixteenth century the gospel-preachers discovered the gospel of the Bible and especially of Paul. They discovered that justification was not at all by our godliness but was by the righteousness of Jesus being reckoned ours. They saw clearly what Paul meant when he said we are not 'justified by the works of the law'. So they rejected the teaching of Aquinas and others that justification comes by a mixture of faith and love and other aspects of godliness, including law-keeping. They said salvation comes by Jesus' righteousness being given to us, and that it is grasped by faith only. However, they accepted Thomas Aquinas' division of the law into three.

The teaching of the gospel-preachers that we are justified only by faith scandalised the Catholics. 'You are saying that we do not have to obey the law of God,' they said. 'Your so-called gospel encourages sin.'

The sixteenth century gospel-preachers replied, 'Well, we are free from the law as a way of justification, but we still have the law (that is Aquinas' moral law) as a way of sanctification.' This idea became dominant and Paul's teaching that we have died to the law *in order to bear fruit to God* (that is, in order to be sanctified!) was missed. It became the habit among Christians to talk about 'the law' but mean only certain bits of the law of Moses (actually less than 1% of it!) and to say it was a 'rule of life' for the Christian.

We now need to ask the question, 'How much of the traditional teaching of the churches has grasped hold of Paul's teaching?' And the answer is: Not much! Most of it is Aquinas more than Paul!

The time is ripe for us to take a step nearer to the Bible

than ever before. We can stand on the shoulders of great men who have preceded us, and we shall learn things they did not see and yet they have helped us. 'The law' is a case in point.

Paul quite clearly teaches that we have died to the law in order to be fruitful towards God. Is 'being fruitful' justification or sanctification? It is sanctification. We died to the law 'in order to live unto God' (Gal. 2:19). Is 'living unto God' justification or sanctification? Clearly these verses say we have died to the law, not just in the matter of justification but with regard to our total relationship to God. Paul makes precisely this point to the Galatians. Having begun with the Spirit, he asks, are you now going back to Mosaic law-keeping? The Galatians were already saved! They were wanting to turn to the Mosaic law as a means of being holy! It is this that Paul denounces as turning back to the flesh.

The truth is: we have to die to the law altogether! We have to relate differently to God if we are to be fruitful, if we are to 'live to God'. At our point in the history of the church we must be ready to go behind Calvin, behind Thomas Aquinas, behind Augustine, and back to Paul, back to Jesus, back to walking in the Spirit. We shall fulfil the law, but we shall do so by walking in the Spirit.

31

CHRIST'S
FULFILLING THE LAW
(Romans 7:4)

In chapter 29 we drew out two principles from Romans 7:4. A third principle in this verse is: *this dying to the law takes place through union with Christ in his body upon the cross.* 'You also died to the law through the body of Christ.'

What does 'also' mean? Is it 'Also—as well as the cases in verses 1–3'? Or 'Also—as well as Jesus who died to sin'? Or 'You Gentiles also as well as we Jews'? I think the 'also' looks back to chapter 6. 'You did not only die to sin. You *also* died to the law.' They died to sin through the death of Jesus (see Romans 6:3–8); they *also* died to the law through the death of Jesus in His body on the cross.

When Jesus died on the cross, He was taking our sins upon Himself. He was also taking the law of Moses upon Himself. He had 'fulfilled the law' (see Matt. 5:17–18). He came 'under the law' (Gal. 4:4). He kept the Mosaic law in minute detail. He obeyed the Sabbath (but not additions to it). He kept its ritual, attended its festivals, offered its sacrifices. He refused to criticise it when invited to. When He changed it (as He did) it was to move in the direction of deeper and higher spirituality (Matt. 5:21–48 has several examples).

But then He fulfilled its picture-language. He was the great high Priest of the law. He was the great Prophet of Deuteronomy 18. He was the King of Deuteronomy 17:15 amidst His brothers.

He fulfilled all the picture-language of the law. He was the meal-offering, the burnt-offering, the peace-offering, the sin-offering, the trespass-offering. He was the Passover lamb. He sprinkled His blood in the heavenly sanctuary.

Not only did He keep all the positive requirements of the law, but at the end He faced the highest punishment of the law.

He took upon Himself the death penalty, the worst punishment the law could hand out. He came under the curse mentioned in Deuteronomy 21:23.

So the law was fully dealt with by Jesus. All the demands of the Mosaic law, and more, all the demands of His Father's holy will, have been met by the body of Jesus hanging on the cross. So I am free from the slightest threat coming from any aspect of the Mosaic law! And any lesser law of any other people or that I can invent myself has also been defeated. I have died in Christ. My marriage to the law has come to an end. It no longer has authority over me. I am no longer united to it. As a Gentile it was never really addressed to me. But Christ was a Jew. He came under it. I died in Him. Whether I am a Jew or not I know that the law can never ever approach me, intimidate me, or give me the slightest fear. I have died to the law through the body of Christ.

This dying to the law leaves me free for a new relationship. *So, my brothers, you also died to the law through the body of Christ, that you might belong to another, to Him who was raised from the dead, in order that we might bear fruit to God.*

Now for a fourth principle. *The Christian is united to Christ; Christ is risen from the dead; so I am risen from the dead in Christ.* I am 'married' to the risen and ascended and enthroned Lord Jesus Christ.

This is the secret of holiness. It is not that I struggle to keep laws. I simply am joined on to my heavenly husband and I live to please Him. And He gives me the motivation, the strength, the joy, that enables me to please Him. Everything that I could not do through one kind of law or another, I can do in Jesus. I could not live a godly life through the Mosaic law. It was a yoke I was not able to bear (see Acts 15:10). I could not cope with Thomas Aquinas' reinterpreted version of it that came to me via my Puritan friends.

But now I am under Jesus. I consult Him every day. He releases me from all my guilty past. And He helps me in all my wobbly present. And He tells me He will stay with me through all my future, come what may.

He began by telling me that all my transgressions were forgiven and forgotten. Then He says to me that if I confess my sins to Him daily, He will forgive me daily. He tells me that if I walk in the light I will have continued fellowship with Him, and that His blood will go on cleansing me from all sins.

Jesus is my heavenly husband. I am in a 'one flesh' relationship with Him. I know I am united to Him. His death is my death and releases me from my past. He is buried, so I am buried. I share His history. I have an intimate relationship to Him. I have to be subject to Him. As a wife is subject to her husband, I have to be subject to Jesus. He makes the final decisions of my life. Although He allows me to have my own mind and often gives me the desires of my heart, yet He is the head in this relationship I have with Him. He is the chairman of all our conversations. I talk to Him. He talks with me. Yet I am conscious that He is often taking the lead in our fellowship together. It is a marriage 'until death do us part', but since He will not die and I will not die, I am His and He is mine for ever. This is how I live, not married to the law, but married to Jesus.

FREE FROM THE LAW
(Romans 7:4)

Paul says *So, my brothers and sisters, you also were made to die to the law through the body of Christ.* People are often afraid of the idea that we have died to the law. The 'natural man' is a legalist, just as the 'natural man' is careless about sin. We are too strict and too loose at the same time! We all tend to feel that if we have a detailed list of regulations about this, that and the other, we shall be safer. There is some truth in this. In certain situations it is good to have things in writing and to have clear principles. The trouble is we go too far, and we get to trust in 'the written code'. Eventually we find that we are not living on the Holy Spirit at all. The Old Covenant originated with a book. From the first day there was a set of writings, the book of the law. But the New Covenant originated with the outpouring of the Spirit. Writing was not indispensably part of it.

We know that godliness is important and we fear that some people (including ourselves!) may get too lawless if they do not have some kind of law. So we think the law of God is needed, possibly in detailed and codified form. Again there is something to be said for this. The apostles eventually put instructions into writing and insisted that their instructions were authoritative and the word of God. They were putting into writing what they knew was the leading of the Spirit.

We hear rumours of people who have gone into terrible sin because they have claimed to be free from the law. There was a wicked monk by the name of Rasputin who lived a vile life, but justified what he did saying he was 'free from the law'. Something similar is true of a cult that was prominent a few years ago. However these incidents are rare. Most scandals do not come from people who claim to be free from the law; they tend to come more from people who want to be under it! But let him who thinks he stands take heed lest he fall. Most of the people who have been reckoned to be lawless in this matter were godly people. In the sixteenth century there was a man called Agricola who opposed the teaching of Luther concerning the law. The word 'antinomian' was coined; it means 'someone whose teaching is opposed to law'. 'Antinomianism' (in the way the word is generally used) means moral looseness, carelessness about sin. People have often had terrible fear of 'antinomians'. Actually Agricola was as godly as Luther! Many people have been called 'antinomians', even when there is not the slightest hint of anything wicked about their lives. People have fallen into legalism and moralism far more often than into antinomianism. Read the books on the subject. Read Tom Torrance's *The Doctrine of Grace in the Apostolic Fathers* or FitzSimons Alison's book, *The Rise of Moralism.* You will discover that the church slides into legalism and moralism more than it slides into easy careless living. Looseness about sin generally arises in those highly moral communities that have forgotten the gospel. Luther complained there was great immorality in the monasteries which had been brought into being in the interests of holiness!

The best way to get an overview of the subject and to get a clear mind on the matter is, I think, to see that every aspect of the law is 'typological'.

Salvation through grace, and godliness through grace, are both without the Mosaic law. The gospel was announced centuries before the law . For several centuries the gospel was preached to Abraham. Promises about the coming 'seed of Abraham' were given. Abraham believed them and was reckoned righteous before God. He was justified before the law existed! He got to a high level of godliness before the law existed.

Then the law was added. It came in afterwards. But it was always a temporary measure. It was added 'until the seed should come'. Now we are no longer under the guardian of the law. The Mosaic law lasts only until the giving of the gospel. Then the interim-law of Moses was finished and the church of Jesus was put back to the position of Abraham. We are children of Abraham, not children of Moses. The law was given 'until Christ came', as most translations translate Galatians 3:24. (The old translation 'to lead us to Christ' is quite wrong. The law does not exactly lead us to Christ, although it shuts out all other possibilities. The Holy Spirit leads us to Christ, and He does not need the Mosaic institutions of the law to do it.) There were various reasons for the giving of the law. It restrained sin. It could be used, when taken spiritually, to bring an intense awareness of the power of sin. But among other things it pictured Jesus. It was a 'type' of the person of Jesus and a 'type' of the righteousness Jesus would bring by the Holy Spirit.

Consider the animal sacrifices. They were 'typological' of Jesus. The five sacrifices each symbolised different aspects of what God demands of His people and of what Jesus would provide. The burnt offering symbolised total consecration. The meal offering symbolised dedication of one's labours. The peace-offering symbolised and typified the fellowship and peace and celebration with others that atonement brings. The sin-offering and guilt-offering typified sin-bearing by a Saviour in its different aspects.

The Christian knows that He does not have to sacrifice an animal. The law is only a 'shadow of the good things to come' (Heb. 10:1) and not the reality itself. The same was true of other aspects of the law. The rules about food and festivals and sabbath days—these are all 'a mere shadow' (Col. 2:17). What is not often not appreciated is that the same thing is true of every aspect of the law. The entire Mosaic system was a shadow of Jesus.

33

THE LAW AS A SHADOW
(Romans 7:4)

Paul says *So, my brothers and sisters, you also were made to die to the law through the body of Christ.*
Consider the following diagram.

PASSOVER ———— 50 DAYS ————→ SINAI

CRUCIFIXION ———— 50 DAYS ————→ PENTECOST

There was a day in the history of Israel when a lamb died for the sins of the people. On the day when the lamb died the people were released from bondage, and were made the people of God. Before the lamb died for them they could not get out of Egypt. After the lamb died for them they could not stay in Egypt.

Fifty days after the people were saved by the blood of the lamb the people of God were given the law through Moses. On that occasion, when the law was given, there were 'lightning flashes' (Exod. 19:16). Jewish rabbis saw the 'lightning flashes' of Exodus 19:16 as tongues of fire going to all the nations. This was all symbolical and 'typological' of Jesus. When Jesus came, He fulfilled the law. It was all pointing to Him. He is the Passover lamb. Again God's people are those who are saved by the blood of the lamb.

Fifty days after Jesus died at a Passover festival, it was the day of Pentecost. It was the day for the celebration of the law. Thousands of Jews were there from many nations. And God acted! Fifty days after the *first* Passover came His law. Now fifty days after the true Passover, comes . . . comes what? The giving of a new law? No. The gift of the Spirit! The Spirit is the replacement of the law. The Spirit is for the New Covenant what the law was for the Old Covenant.

Now here is the thing that is often not realised. The whole of the Mosaic law was 'typological' of the coming of Jesus—including the so-called moral law! This point is easily grasped in connection with animal sacrifices but it is not so easily seen with regard to what is called the 'moral law'.

For the Christian to go back to animal sacrifices or back to circumcision or back to the keeping of obligatory holy days, is all a waste of time. It is false teaching.

But here is a point not always appreciated. Even the so-called 'moral' laws are also only a pale shadow of the spirituality Jesus requires. We have 'died to the law' in every respect. We have died to the law with regard to its moral commands, not in order to sin, but in order to be placed under something higher. People who fear that 'dying to the law' leads to sin have not got the point. The Spirit is higher than the law! The Sermon on the Mount is higher than the law. And the Sermon on the Mount is not an exposition of the law.

Are we free from the Ten Commandments? That is like the old question 'Have you stopped beating your wife?' You are in trouble if you say yes, and you are in trouble if you say no! The best thing is to reject the question!

The fact is we are not under the Ten Commandments because the Ten Commandments are only a feeble pale shadow of what we are under. We do not kill animals because the sacrifice of Jesus is greater. Take the command 'You shall not steal'. Is the Christian under it? He certainly is to keep it. But if that is all he bothers about it will hold him down to a low level of spirituality. He will be happy that he has not stolen and that will be the end of the matter.

But Paul, putting into words the leading of the Spirit, says, 'Let him that stole steal no more' (Eph. 4:28). That gets about as far as the Ten Commandments got. It is restricted to stealing; it is negative in form. If Paul had stopped there he would in effect have been repeating one of the Ten Commandments. But actually Paul did not draw attention to the fact that what he was saying was similar to the law, and he went on to go much further than the eighth of the Ten Commandments. He went on to the positive leading of the Spirit ' . . . let him labour, performing with his own hands what is good'. Then he went on to give Christian motives, the kind of motivation the Holy Spirit puts before us. The Christian must positively earn something 'in order that he may have something to share with him who is in need'. The original law was only a pale shadow of the kind of leading that the Holy Spirit will give.

Jesus says He comes to 'fulfil' the law. This does not mean simply to put us under it! It means to work in us so that the Spirit leads us in a way that goes beyond obeying the letter of moral regulations. The Spirit leads us into ways that were not even mentioned in the law.

The fact is the moral law is *also* only a shadow. When Paul says we have died to the law. Just as we do not focus on animal sacrifices, nor do we focus on the regulations of the Mosaic covenant as though they could give us much help. What do we do then? We pray. We ask ourselves the question, 'What is the pathway of love in this situation I am in?' As we do that the Spirit will lead us. We ask the question, 'What would I like him to do for me if the situation were reversed?' (see Matt. 7:12). The Spirit will lead us and He will vastly outstrip the vast majority of the regulations of the law. The Spirit's leading can overtake and improve on almost everything in the law. I say 'Almost' because the Spirit will not improve on Leviticus 19:18, 'You shall love your neighbour as yourself.' If you want to be under the law, be under that bit! The Holy Spirit will show you how. And you will not break the morality of the law, but you will go beyond it.

34

UNION WITH JESUS
(Romans 7:4)

Dying to the law takes place through union with Christ in His body upon the cross. The Christian is united to Christ; Christ is risen from the dead; so I am risen from the dead in Christ.

It does not mean that the Christian has died to morality! It does not mean that he has died to righteousness or to godliness. But it means that he has died to the entire system of law that was given to Moses upon Mount Sinai in the thirteenth or fifteenth century BC (scholars argue about the date!)

Paul is simply reapplying the teaching he gave in Romans chapter 6 about being placed into union with Christ. Jesus died; I died in Him. Jesus rose from the dead; I rose from being spiritually dead and cut off from God. I am now joined on to Jesus. I am married to Him. I am seated in the heavenly places.

The gospel-preachers of the sixteenth century, Luther and Calvin, were often criticised for being against morality. The charge was nonsense, but it came because of their teaching (and the Bible's teaching) that salvation was without works. They taught that, 'We have died to the law so far as justification is concerned but we have not died to it so far as sanctification is concerned.' They were trying to refute the charge that they were careless about godliness.

Reformation theologians divided the law into civic, ceremonial and moral sections. They were ex-Roman Catholics and were still following Aquinas at this point. They tended to say the law had three purposes. It had (they said) a political use, and was intended to restrain sin out of fear of punishment. (ii) It had (they said) a humbling use, and was intended to convict of sin, and (iii) they said it had an educational use and was intended to guide the godly man into godliness. The first of these points is certainly right. It is what Paul says in Galatians 3:19. The second and third are dubious. In all of this they were not so much thinking of the 2000 and more verses of legislation in Exodus, Leviticus, Numbers and Deuteronomy. They were more thinking of the idea of the 'moral law' which they had inherited from Aquinas. All of this is needs rethinking. Modern New Testament scholars of all persuasions are more or less agreed that Paul did not teach that the law was a 'rule of life'.

But let's go back to Paul. *So, my brothers, you also died to the law through the body of Christ, that you might belong to another, to Him who was raised from the dead, in order that we might bear fruit to God.*

The Christian is 'married' to Jesus. Being a Christian is a matter of getting united to Jesus Christ. When we put our trust in Jesus, it is not simply an intellectual matter. It is when the Spirit has gripped us, when we are 'poured into the mould' (Rom. 6:17) of God's gospel. We get intimately bound together with our Lord Jesus Christ. We are His people from that point on. We have died to what we were. We have left everything to belong to Him. We have His status before God. We share His position. When a man becomes a King, his wife becomes a Queen! If Jesus is King of Kings and Lord of Lords, and I am married to Him, then what a powerful, rich, abundant, privileged position I am in. I have Jesus' righteousness, Jesus' wisdom, Jesus's sanctification. When Jesus comes in His Second Coming, I shall be with Him. He is my heavenly Lord.

Because I am married to Jesus I have right of access to Him. I can call upon His help at any time. I can bring all my needs to Him. I have His angels quietly and secretly working on my behalf without my even being aware of it. They are His angels, but I am married to Him, so they are my angels too.

Because I am married to Him, I live for Him. It is not just a matter of being under the Mosaic law, not even a matter of being 'moral'. It is a matter of positively living for the praise of my heavenly husband, wanting His honour, wanting to please Him. My beloved is mine and I am His.

Unlike the law He speaks to me in terms of love and grace and mercy and kindness. Just as a husband guides and supports and cherishes his wife, so Jesus cherishes me. So my growing in holiness is responsiveness. What does a husband want more than anything else in a wife? Responsiveness. A feeling of rapport. He wants things to be such that at the raising of an eyebrow his loved one smiles back at him. Jesus wants to be in a love-relationship with us such that we respond to Him.

He wants us ourselves. Putting it practically, Jesus wants our companionship in our talking to Him, sharing with Him.

My growing in holiness is loving submission. If Jesus guides me in tender love, I respond back towards Jesus. I get ready for companionship. Jesus purifies His bride that He might be united to her. He is the spotless, pure one. He wants His bride to be as pure as He is. Marriage when it is truly as it ought to be is the highest form of companionship.

My growing in holiness is zeal that Jesus' plans for me should be fulfilled. Surely a bride is passionately in love with her husband. She identifies with him closely in everything. She wants to share his mind, his ambitions, his future, his everything. I am not under the law, I am married to Jesus!

35

FRUITFULNESS WITHOUT THE LAW
(Romans 7:4)

I am putting Paul's teaching over against the teaching that has become traditional in some parts of the church.

The 'Reformation' approach to law, inherited from Aquinas, was intensified by the British and American Puritans of the seventeenth century. The doctrine of the 'law' that is in the Westminster Confession of Faith, published in 1646, is typical. We ought to know about it if we are to understand the view of the law that most Christians have inherited.

1. They read the law back into the Garden of Eden. They said that Adam was under it and Abraham was under it (contradicting Romans 5:14!)

2. They said the law was perfect, eternal, a reflection of God Himself.

3. They followed Aquinas in dividing it into three, two parts of which they said have expired or are abrogated.

4. They said the moral law was a guide to the Christian, 'directing and binding everyone'.

5. They interpreted the law by 'spiritualising' it. They were not content with the straightforward meaning of the laws of Exodus to Deuteronomy.

6. They turned the negative form of most of the Ten Commandments into positive form, turning 'You shall not' into 'You shall'.

7. They extended the commandments, giving lists of sins forbidden or duties required by each command.

One comment must suffice. The Puritan focus was on regulations and legal guidelines. Paul's focus is on directly living by the Holy Spirit, which (he says) will lead to the law being fulfilled anyway. Paul's teaching is that if we walk in the Spirit deliberately, we shall fulfil the law accidentally! He says

we died to the law (all of it!) but this is 'so that the righteous
requirement of the law might be fulfilled in . . . ' In whom?   In
which people does the righteous requirement get fulfilled and
how does it happen? He goes on ' . . . in us who walk not after
the flesh but according to the Spirit' (Rom. 8:4). It is walking in
the Spirit that gets the requirements of the law truly fulfilled. It
achieves what the law was striving after and pointing to. But
being under the law directly, leads to legalism, depression,
heaviness of Spirit. (However, I have to say the Puritans were
great people and often their spiritual instincts were better than
the traditions they inherited from Aquinas!)

Paul is more radical than the sixteenth- and seventeenth-
century theologians. He says that we have died to the law with
regard to sanctification as well as with regard to justification.
'You have died to the law . . . in order to bear fruit for God.'

I ought to mention that in recent years there have been a
few people who have even taught that we have to bring back the
judicial and civic aspects of the Mosaic law. They call it
'theonomy'. They think civil magistrates should be applying the
law of Moses and that the civil laws of the thirteenth century BC
in Israel are a model of perfect social justice. They talk of the
abiding validity of the Mosaic law in exhaustive detail.
Homosexuals and juvenile delinquents should be executed! The
jubilee year should be brought back! And so on.

In my opinion all of this is quite unscriptural. Even at a
national civic level we can go beyond the law of Moses. Would
Wilberforce have abolished slavery if he had been following the
law? We can *learn* from the political aspects of the law God gave
to Israel. That is not the same as saying we can simply apply it to
modern societies, and that it cannot be improved upon.

What is surprising is that some charismatic people have
been drawn to theonomy. This is quite amazing and shows how
weak the charismatic movement—of which I am a member—is in
its doctrinal understanding! Pentecostals and theonomy! The
friends of the Holy Spirit and the friends of the law! It is like
marrying a dove (the Holy Spirit!) to a rhinoceros (the law!).

The truth of the matter is we have died to the entire
Mosaic system. It is not enough to take Paul to mean died 'to
the *guilt* of the law'. Paul's whole argument is dealing with
godly living. Bearing fruit to God is not justification; it is
sanctification. Paul is saying we have to be released from the law
in order to live a holy life. People have often been happy about

saying we die to the law to be justified, but have been unhappy about saying we die to the law to get sanctified. But the latter is precisely what Paul is saying!

A final point in connection with Romans 7:4 is this: (5) *The union that the Christian has with Jesus produces fruit.* It is the 'fruit' of a new position, where we are able to rejoice in the Lord, where we are confident that our loving heavenly husband will bring us to be all that He wants us to be.

It is the 'fruit' of godliness in our character and disposition: love, joy, peacefulness, patience, kindness, goodness, faithfulness, meekness, self-control.

It is the fruit of achieving something for God, having an impact upon our world.

No amount of strict observance of law is likely to lead to great fruitfulness. Those who have achieved much for God have been people who have rejoiced in their close relationship to Jesus. It was not the legalism of our spiritual forefathers that enabled them to serve God. It was their loving responsiveness to Jesus. We ought to be able to live unto our heavenly husband and reach greater heights of spiritual fruitfulness. His strength is so great that even in people like us He is able to bear fruit for the glory of His Father.

36

LIFE UNDER LAW
(Romans 7:5)

At this point Paul's argument takes a step forward. He now wants to compare and contrast two ways of life, the way of living in the flesh (7:5) and the way of living in the Holy Spirit.

For when we were in the flesh, the sinful passions aroused by the law were at work in our bodies, so that we bore fruit for death. But now, by dying to what once bound us, we have been released from the law so that we serve in the new way of the Spirit, and not in the old way of the written code (7:5–6). Consider the differences between the old life and the new life.

1. Consider what was controlling the two lives. One was 'in the flesh'; the other is 'in the newness of the Spirit'.

2. Consider the time involved. One was the past unregenerate life ('we were'); the other is the present life of the Christian ('But now . . . ').

3. Consider the power of the law involved. In one it was a case of 'sinful passions aroused by the law . . . at work in our bodies . . . '; in the other situation we are 'released from the law . . . '.

4. Consider the fruit involved. In the one case it is 'fruit for death'; in the other (as Paul has told us before) it is 'fruit for God' (7:4).

5. In one it is 'oldness'; in the other it is 'newness'.

Let us look at verse 5 and life under the law.

(1) *He is referring to the unconverted time of life:* 'when we were in the flesh'. 'The flesh' is the realm of human sinfulness. To be 'in' the flesh is to be ruled by sinfulness. We were all once 'in the flesh', ruled by sinfulness, unable to please God (see Rom. 8:8).

(2) *Paul, and the Roman Christians, were at that time under the law.* Paul uses the word 'we'. He is referring to himself and people who for one reason or another were like himself. The law is not a general moral code that everyone is under. It is rather

the law that God gave at Sinai to Israel. But in one way or another Paul can say that 'we'—I and many of you Romans like me—were under the law.

'Flesh' and 'law' go together. People who think they can relate to God by way of law are actually trusting the flesh, the sinful nature. The Galatians had been saved by the preaching of the cross of Jesus, and they had learned to live by the Holy Spirit. One day they listened to legalists and turned to law. Paul says 'Having begun with the Spirit, are you now being perfected by the flesh?' (Gal. 3:3). To the Philippians he wrote, 'We put no confidence in the flesh' and went on to explain how he had once put trust in law but did so no longer (Phil. 3:3–9). 'Trust' in law is trust in 'flesh', the weak sinful human nature. Most people live like this. They trust in themselves and feel capable of keeping God's law or their own laws. But all of that is trust in the flesh. Again it is clear that he is referring to the unregenerate pre-Christian time of life.

(3) *The Mosaic law did not help Paul in these unconverted days; it inflamed sin in him, and in others like him.* Paul says 'when we were in the flesh, the sinful passions aroused by the law were at work in our bodies . . . '

Men and women have 'sinful desires'. This refers to our natural appetites, but they get out of hand and become excessive. They rule us. We are not controlled by our intelligence; we are controlled by what we *want* ruling our mind and our decisions.

These desires of ours which get out of control and become sinful get 'aroused by the law'. Any kind of law actually arouses our sinfulness. One might think that law controls sin. It may do so if the threat of punishment is great! But at the same time as law may or may not curb sin, it actually increases the desire for sin.

This sin is aroused and inflamed in our 'members', the parts of our bodies. We have seen before that sin resides in the human nature in our fallen bodies. This includes our brain, our sexuality, our desires for comfort, our imaginations, every part of our physical make-up.

(4) *Life under the law produces death.* The end of the whole procedure is the God-less-ness which is death. It produces guilt. It separates us from God even more. It produces coldness, a sense of failure, despair. Life under the law is nothing but dust and ashes! The law cannot help us in any deep way. It does not justify, it does not regenerate, it does not sanctify. It leads to

deeper and deeper despair, that Paul summarises in one word, 'death'.

Thank God for verse 6. Verse 5 is not the end of the story. Paul is able to go on to say, 'But now . . . !' These words are always wonderful words. When we are in the depths of despair God has a habit of butting in! Coming to know Jesus Christ as our Saviour is not a small matter. It is a gigantic leap from sin and death and despair to life and newness and power.

The reason why Paul is describing despair under the law was so that he might go on to say, 'But . . .'

When a person believes in Jesus Christ, he or she is taken out of this realm of sin and judgement and law altogether, and is given the Holy Spirit. It is an entirely new realm, a realm 'in Christ' and under grace. Where sin once abounded now grace abounds all the more. The Christian is to get hold of the fact. He has died to the law; he is in the Spirit for ever.

37

OLDNESS IS COLDNESS
(Romans 7:6)

Paul has described what it is like to be an unconverted person, under the law. Now he puts the other side of the comparison. But now, by dying to what once bound us, we have been released from the law so that we serve in the new way of the Spirit, and not in the old way of the written code.

When Jesus died, He released all believers from the law and even from the slightest threat of the law.

Israel served God via the law. That way of God has a tendency to be impersonal. True, it was possible for believers in those days to read the five books of the law and hear the voice of our heavenly Father. That would be part of what the psalmists meant when they say they delight in the written teaching of the law. However when one's focus is on obedience to the written legislation of the Mosaic covenant, there is a strong tendency to forget about the Holy Spirit and focus on the writing. But 'the letter kills'. There is a strong tendency for the letter, even the letter of the Scriptures, to displace the Holy Spirit. The Bible was never written to displace or replace the Holy Spirit. If we focus on the Holy Spirit and on personal fellowship with our heavenly Father, He often lifts us up to heights of joy and fellowship. In such fellowship we surpass the letter of the covenant of law given on Mount Sinai to Israel.

The law—all the institutions of Israel given at the time of Moses recorded for us in about 1500 verses of legislation—is characterised by 'the old way of the written code'.

'The written code' is old. This not only means that it has been around for a long time. It also means that there is something fixed about it. The law does not change. It does not have anything fresh about it.

The law is written. It is codified. It is not so much a person speaking to us as a book being given to us. It tends to be impersonal. Obedience is the application of these written commands that we study. It is outside of us. You had to look at it with your physical eyes and seek to obey it. There is not necessarily anything wrong with reading a book! But while you are reading a book you are not talking to a person. The Pharisees spent a lot of time reading the law, but they did not have much contact with the living God.

Oldness is coldness. There is something cold and dry about trying to live a life for God upon the basis of law. There is no warmth in it. It is the opposite of what happened on the road to Emmaus, when the disciples talked with the living Lord Jesus and said later, 'Did not our hearts burn within us?'

When you are living by legislation, you are in control of the situation and the lawbook is in control of you. There is a fixedness about the entire process. There is no flexibility. It is not that you are led this way one day but another way in a different situation. It is not that God leads you one way but takes into account the needs of people and leads another person differently. No, everything about the law is fixed, inflexible, predictable.

Legislation tends to remove the need for guidance. No one in Israel ever prayed about when Passover should be. It was fixed. They only argued about the interpretation of the law! There is no need to pray for guidance about something where there is a fixed and written law.

Law produces a judgemental atmosphere. It tends to condemn you, and you condemn everyone else. The law had no forgiveness for any serious sins. It did not have much of an atmosphere for forgiveness in it. The blood of the sacrifices could only forgive minor matters. So law tends to produce a guilt-laden atmosphere.

If the law was viewed so spiritually that notice was taken about internal matters and the tenth commandment, the atmosphere of judgement was even worse, for the law viewed in such a way could only condemn.

Paul has one word for all of this: death! The law kills!

However, the Christian gospel is the entire reverse of all of this. The Spirit is newness. The love-command is the 'new commandment'. It is flexible. It is the Spirit personally leading us day by day into ways of love. The leading of the Spirit is not written, it is internal. It is a person speaking to us. It is warmth; the Spirit is a mighty rushing wind. He is burning fire.

When the Spirit is at work you are not in control. You are never quite sure what is going to happen. And if you *can* totally control the manifestations of the Spirit, it is more likely manipulation than really the Spirit. There is flexibility with the Spirit. God does take into account the needs of people and the needs of varying situations. We seek the personal guidance of our heavenly Father. He does not ever contradict the righteousness of the law but His personal guidance is more intimate. The Spirit is our Advocate, our counsellor beside us. Prayer is the very heartbeat of life in the Holy Spirit. Jesus never brings a judgemental atmosphere. Jesus shows us His love, reveals His wonderful purposes for us, whispers His love into our hearts, gives us hopes and glimpses of glory, gives us joy and new power. None of this is found in the law. It only comes by direct relationship to Jesus and by serving God in the Spirit.

38

THE NEWNESS OF THE SPIRIT
(Romans 7:6)

By dying to what once bound us, the law, we serve God in the new way of the Spirit.

The Christian life is a life lived in the power and blessing of the Holy Spirit. It is not a matter of bookish legislation. Even the gospel and its teaching must never be allowed to become bookish legislation!

What is this 'newness of the Spirit' like? It begins with the experience of the Holy Spirit. I deliberately use the word 'experience'. In the New Testament Christians received the Holy Spirit in a way that they were aware of. You did not need to prove to them that they had the Holy Spirit!

There is more than one aspect to the work of the Holy Spirit at the time people come to Jesus Christ. There is a hidden, secret work of the Spirit, as He gets people to see the truth about Jesus. When a person believes, the Spirit has been that person's inner teacher even if he is unaware of how he knows the truth.

But there is also an *experience* of the Spirit. It is this experiential aspect of the Spirit's work that starts the Christian life off with a mighty leap forward. It is 'receiving power' (Acts 1:8). It is knowing that we are children of God and crying 'Abba, Father' (Rom. 8:16). It is joy unspeakable and full of glory (1 Pet. 1:8). It is the end of being thirsty (Isa. 44:3). It gives assurance of sonship (Isa. 44:5), ends the hiding of God's face (Ezek. 39:29). It leads to enlargement of gifts of understanding and of speech (Joel 2:28, 29). It is a profuse and abundant matter, a baptism, a deluge, rivers of living water, floods upon the dry ground. It brings illumination, glimpses of the glory of Jesus (John 14:26; 15:26), enjoyment of the love of God (Rom. 5:5), foretastes of heaven. It may be recalled as a conscious experience some years later.

This is just the start. Conscious enjoyment of the Holy Spirit comes right at the very beginning of the Christian life.

True, it may be later than conversion, but that is a great abnormality judged by the New Testament. Every Christian should know the Holy Spirit in this way from early days in his life as a Christian.

Then the Holy Spirit sprinkles and saturates every aspect of the Christian life. It is a matter of serving God in the new way of the Spirit from that point onwards.

The Spirit gives understanding and illumination. God reveals things by the Spirit (1 Cor. 2:10). We are not under the law, we are under the Spirit. In this personal one-to-one, internal, fellowship with God, we get taught and guided and helped along. The veil is taken away (2 Cor. 3:16). We are able to look boldly into the face of Jesus and know that He loves us and is smiling upon us. God makes His light shine in our hearts.

The Spirit gives us assurance. It is not just assurance at the time of our conversion, but permanent on-going day-by-day consciousness that we are the children of God.

The Spirit leads us into love. He produces fruit in us. He speaks to us and we listen and find that again and again He is calling us to love. When we heed Him, He takes us beyond the Mosaic law into the pathways of affection. Then when we heed His call to love, all sorts of other beautiful things appear with love: joy, peace, patience, and sweet beautiful tenderness in a dozen ways.

We are not under the law; we are led by the Holy Spirit. If we are led by the Holy Spirit we are not under the law because we do not need to be! He enables us to mortify the sinful inclinations we find within ourselves because we are still in the body (Rom. 8:13). He gives us strength and encouragement (Acts 9:31). He supplies us with 'joy given by the Holy Spirit' (1 Thess. 1:6). It is difficult to live a godly life under the law. It is not so difficult when we are rejoicing in the Holy Spirit. The very heart of the kingdom of God is 'joy in the Holy Spirit' (Rom. 14:17) and it is this that works holiness into our lives even unconsciously and without Pharisaism.

The Holy Spirit is one who 'anoints' everything in the Christian life. 'Anointing' is a piece of picture language. It means to apply oil or lubrication. This is the heart of what life in the Holy Spirit is like. It is lubricated! It flows. Oil makes things flow smoothly. You put oil in grinding wheels, on squeaky hinges, on grating machines. After the oil has been applied, everything flows smoothly. So it is in the Christian life.

Law is laborious and heavy and often onerous. But under the lubrication of the Holy Spirit Jesus's commands to love everyone everywhere are not grievous. They are enjoyable! There is a lubrication about what we do for God. The wheels of the Christian life spin round smoothly when the Holy Spirit is giving us a sense of the personal presence of Jesus. The hinges turn nicely. The procedures flow. Fellowship is rich and wonderful. Burdens are lifted. Worship is exhilarating.

None of this comes through the law! True, there is conflict in the Christian life. There will be times of suffering, for it is through many tribulations that we experience the blessings of God's kingdom. But still the Spirit is with us. The 'Spirit of glory and of God' rests upon us when we are rejoicing in fellowship with Jesus. If we suffer as a Christian, we praise God that we bear the name of Christ upon us. The kingdom of God is joy in the Holy Spirit.

39

THE SPIRIT IN THE CHURCH
(Romans 7:6)

No spiritual power ever comes to us by our being under the law. None of the blessings of the gospel come to us by means of any ordinance of the covenant of law that God imposed on Israel upon Mount Sinai. None of the distinctives of this covenant have any obligation in the New Covenant. Holy buildings, holy days, special calendars, circumcision, rules about food, about tribes, religious festivals—and a mass of other things—will never enable us to serve God with power. The moral commands of the Ten Commandments—or nine of them, minus the Saturday sabbath—are nowhere near high enough for us to please God through them. Even less are we helped by the law's most sharp and powerful command: you shall not covet.

We serve God in an entirely different way. By dying to what once bound us, the law, we serve God in the new way of the Spirit.

Another aspect of this life in the Holy Spirit is that the flowing and beautiful anointing of the Spirit is at work in the church. The Christian is not allowed by the Spirit to be an isolated creature, a loner. He brings us into the church and blesses us there also. It is the Holy Spirit who put us in the church in the first place. He immersed us into the body of Christ (1 Cor. 12:13). From that point on we begin to enjoy the 'fellowship of the Spirit'. We enjoy rich friendship if we are following the leading of the Spirit. He will give us people to share with. His commands always revolve around people. The commands of legislation are often negative and simply restrain us from hurting others as much as we might if left unrestrained. The commands of law stop us murdering, stealing, lying. These things involve people. The commands of the Spirit will always revolve around one central command, the command to love.

Then there will be corporate directives of the Spirit. Perhaps one day we shall be praying with a company of

Christians. As it was in the book of Acts, 'while they were worshipping the Lord and fasting, the Holy Spirit spoke' (Acts 13:2). It was not that Paul had a personal instruction from the Holy Spirit. The Spirit was leading the church as its prophets and teachers prayed.

Then the commands of the Spirit will involve the gifts of the Spirit. How far removed all of this is from the Mosaic law! The Spirit can give gifts of utterance of various kinds, gifts of knowledge, gifts of healing. The greatest of all His gifts is the gift of prophecy, being given what to say by God in a way that speaks piercingly to the needs of the people of God.

The commands of God will lead us into serving people, loving people, reaching people, encouraging people. God will command and enable at the same time. Some will be called to teach. Some will be called to serve with gifts of administration. These will come as commands, as strong directives. It has nothing to do with the law at all. It is all part of the new life of the Spirit. Some people will be called to be 'helps'. Some will have gifts of mercy.

Christian godliness is not obedience to the Mosaic law; it is obedience to the Spirit. It is a matter of not grieving the Spirit (Eph. 4:30), not quenching the Spirit (1 Thess. 5:19), not resisting the Spirit (Acts 7:51), not lying to the Spirit or testing the Spirit (Acts 5:3, 9), not angering the Spirit or despising the Spirit (Isa. 63:10; Heb. 10:29). Instead we walk in the Spirit and sow to the Spirit and are on fire with the Spirit and go on being filled with the Spirit (Gal. 5:16, 18; Rom. 12:11; Eph. 5:18). None of this is to be found in the law and you will not come to it by law-keeping.

Then there is prayer. The commands of the Spirit are likely to have a lot to do with prayer. We are told to 'pray in the Spirit'. There is even non-rational prayer where we do not know precisely what it is that we are praying and yet we have groanings of syllables given to us by the Holy Spirit.

This too is far removed from the legislation of the covenant given to Israel. The law scarcely requires a lot of praying. Praying is hard to find in any of the legislation of the books of Moses. Moses himself was a great man of prayer. He would spend much time with God pleading for the people of Israel. The Lord would speak to Moses face to face, as a man speaks to his friend. But none of this ever got into the law. Moses was not writing his own ideas. The law was being given to him, and God did not tell him to put any instructions in the law about prayer. But the Spirit will call us to prayer again and again.

Then there is music! The Spirit will lead us into music. He will put songs into our hearts. He will fill us with melody and give tunes and words and harmony. Obeying the law will never make you sing a single note! But to be full of the Spirit will lead into worship. There will be singing and joy and praise. The law does not very much require this of you. David was going far beyond the law when he brought choirs and instruments into Israel, and wrote psalms for the people to sing. He was not obeying the law when he did these things. The Spirit was leading David to go beyond the law and higher than the law. David was even then serving God in the new life of the Spirit.

40

CAN THE LAW BE KEPT?
(Romans 7:7)

Everything Paul has said about the law of God so far has been negative and seemingly critical. It brings experience of sin (3:20), it increases sin (5:20), to be under law is the opposite of being under grace (6:14), law inflames sin (7:5). One might be forgiven for thinking that Paul regards the law as coming from the devil! He has actually described law in precisely the same way he has described sin. He has said we died to sin (Rom. 6); he has said we died to the law (Rom. 7:1–4). This leads to an obvious question, 'Is the law sin?' If we have to die to sin and we have to die to the law, are they the same thing? Is the law a sinful and wicked thing? It seems to be on the side of sin and death and judgement. Maybe it is sinful itself? You can see why Paul has reached the point where he has to ask this question. He raises the query and (as before in 6:1 and 6:15) gives a sharp dogmatic answer. *What shall we say then? Is the law sin? Let it not be!*

He asks his question (7:7a) and gives his answer (7:7b). Then he puts forward what I shall call his counter-proposal (7:7c). *But I would not have experienced sin except through the law.*

Paul has already spoken (in 7:5) of the way the law heightens and intensifies sin. He told us in 7:5 that this was an experience that came to him when he was 'in the flesh'. Paul now uses identically the same language here. This shows that he is referring to his pre-conversion experience. There was a time— he says—when I was under the law. It led me into an intense experience of how powerful sin is. He has already said that *Christian* experience is one of *release* from the law (7:6).

The word Paul uses here, often translated 'know', is best translated 'experience' ('I would not have *experienced* sin'). The way the passage develops shows that he deals not with *detached* knowledge 'about' sin, but with intensified experience of sin induced by the law.

It does not mean that intensified experience of sin does not come in any other way. Abraham must have known conviction of sin. We must remember that Scripture says it is the Holy Spirit who convicts of sin. It does not necessitate the Mosaic law.

In what I can call verse 7d Paul starts to explain how he came to experience despair under the law in the days of his flesh. At this point Paul introduces the Tenth Commandment. *For I had not known covetousness if the law had not said 'You shall not covet'.*

This introduces us to a vital point. There are two ways of taking the law of God. The law may be taken externally and it may also be considered with special reference to 'covetousness'.

Before we get into Paul's details, let us consider the giving of the Mosaic law (Exodus to Numbers) *without* reference to covetousness. We shall discover some surprising things. In the story of the first giving of the law it is a fact that the legislation never deals with the 'heart'. In the strictly legislative verses the word never occurs. The references to 'heart' come quite often in the narrative, and in snippets of narrative within the laws, but never in the legislation itself. Leaving aside the Tenth Commandment, the law was not designed to deal with the inward nature of humankind at all. Other than the Tenth Commandment there is nothing in the original version of the law, given on Sinai, that has any regulations about 'the heart' of anyone. We remember the sin of Pharaoh; he hardened his heart again and again. One might think that the law given fifty days later would condemn having a hard heart—but it never did!

This means that the law can be kept! There are plenty of people who do not murder, do not steal, do not lie. Plenty of unconverted people have sufficient morality to get to that level of righteousness. At this level (without considering the Tenth Commandment) *the law can be kept!* The idea is common that it is quite impossible to keep the Mosaic law. Yet if one leaves aside the Tenth Commandment, the law makes the constant assumption that it may be kept. Blessing follows when it is obeyed: 'the man who obeys them will live by them' (Lev. 18:5; cf. Ezek. 20:11, 21; Neh. 9:29). The 'life' promised in the law must not be equated with the 'eternal life' of the New Testament and refers to national stability, longevity and prosperity, not to the fullness of the Spirit and the expectation of heaven. Nevertheless blessing is promised through the keeping of the law. Only when there is a concentration on the Tenth Commandment is there any hint that the law cannot be kept. Otherwise no such hint is found anywhere in Exodus to Numbers.

The unregenerate person without faith may keep the law to a certain extent. This is the point of Paul's remark in Philippians 3:6. Paul, *before* his Damascus road experience, believed that he kept the law. Reflecting upon his Pharisaic experience does not make him speak of his inability to keep the law; rather he speaks of his ability to keep the law. All of this means that the law may be kept *without faith*. 'The law is not of faith,' says Paul. This is one reason why the law is not the standard for the Christian. From one angle it brings about despair (as we shall see in the rest of Romans 7). But looked at from another angle it is too easy; even unconverted people can keep it.

41

IS THE LAW SIN?
(Romans 7:7)

Is the law a sinful and wicked thing? No. If we understand the Tenth Commandment we shall see how deeply and powerful opposed the law is to sin, how it searches into the very depth of human sinfulness.

In its *first* presentation the law was given as something that could be kept. It had to be this way. The law was administered by judges in Israel. It did not demand perfection. What would be the use of a *national* law that demanded we be as sinless as Jesus? Imagine *national* laws that sentence you to banishment from the presence of God if you are an unbeliever! How could it function as a guide to legislation for a nation? Imagine judges who had to judge the state of your heart and sentence you if you were backsliding!

If you read the story that runs from Genesis to Numbers you find that, beginning at Exodus 15:22, chunks of legislation start coming into the story. The legislation comes in about 2000 verses, about 1500 referring to the original giving of the law (Exodus to Numbers). When Moses preached his sermons to Israel on the edge of the promised land, he included slabs of detailed legislation, summarising and sometimes reapplying the earlier legislation (Deut. 5:1—26:19). About another 500 verses of legislation occur in the central sections of Deuteronomy.

A fairly complete list of the original laws is Exodus 12:1–11, 14–20, 24–27, 43–49; 13:1–13; 16:4–5, 23, 25–26, 28, 33; 20:1–17, 22–26; 21:1—23:33; 25:1—31:17; 34:11–26; 35:1–3; Leviticus 1:1—7:34; 11:1—24:9; 25:1—27:34; Numbers 3:5–10, 25–26, 28b, 31, 36; 4:4–33; 5:1—6:21; 15:1–41; 18:1—19:22; 28:1—30:16; 35:1–34.

Try reading it! You will see why the Christian is not 'under the law'. It does not even tell you to pray. It is not really appropriate for the Christian living in the Spirit. The law was not like New Testament appeals for holiness, and New Testament appeals for holiness scarcely use the Mosaic law. In all of the appeals for holiness only Ephesians 6:1–4 refers to the law, and the point there is to urge that the fullness of the Spirit (Eph. 5:18–21) leads to godliness (Eph. 5:22—6:9), and it is the kind of godliness that fulfils the law. Ephesians 6:1–4 is making the same point as Romans 8:2–4. The life of the Spirit fulfils the law.

But otherwise the New Testament appeals for holiness make no reference to the *details* of the law. They refer only to its general appeal for holiness (1 Pet. 19, and the like) and for love (Jas. 2:8 and the like).

The law was administered by magistrates. They could not judge the heart. They could only judge the external behaviour. There had to be witnesses to prove that you had broken the law.

However, there was a deeper way to take the law. The law contained 'ten words', 'ten principles' that put it all in summary form. At the end of the 'Ten Commandments' there was this one: you shall not covet. The word 'covet' simply means 'want' or 'desire'. The Tenth Command looked back over the previous nine and said, 'Not only must you not sin; you must not even want to sin.' Not only must you not commit adultery, you must not want your neighbour's wife. Not only must you not steal, you must not even want your neighbour's ox or donkey. Not only must you not murder, you must not look at anyone else with the slightest degree of animosity; you must not want anything that is his.

It was this command, and this command only that showed the law could be taken to refer to the heart after all. It was to be administered by magistrates, but there was this one line in it that showed the real need was for a heart that did not even want to sin.

It seems to have been Moses himself who first noticed it. Forty years after the giving of the law, when Israel was on the edge of the promised land, Moses gave a series of sermons to the entire nation. Amongst other things he reviewed the way God had led Israel, and he went over the law that God had given them. In the original giving of the law the word 'heart' does not occur in the legislation. But when Moses preached his sermons about the law, he used the word frequently. 'Oh, that their hearts would be inclined to fear me . . . ' 'Love the LORD with all your heart'. 'These words . . . shall be in your heart' (Deut. 5:29; 6:5, 6). Moses said the very thing you might have expected to come in the law itself. 'You shall not harden your heart' (Deut. 15:7). It was Moses who first saw that the law could be applied to the heart, and he preached on it that way forty years after God had given him the law. But none of that was in the law itself—except in the Tenth Commandment! Paul's argument here in Romans 7:7–25 would be ridiculous if it were not for the Tenth Commandment. When Paul said, 'The evil I do not want to do is what I keep on doing', he was not talking about the kind of murder or lying or stealing a judge could throw you into prison for. He was dealing with the heart. It was the Tenth Command, and the Tenth Command only that could function in this way. But when he tried to live such a godly life as not to want to commit any sin of wanting anything evil, he discovered the exceeding sinfulness of sin.

42

EXPERIENCING SIN
(Romans 7:7–9)

It is the Tenth Command only that Paul is referring to from this point on to the end of the chapter 7 of the letter to the Romans. *For I had not known covetousness if the law had not said 'You shall not covet'.*

He is still explaining verse 5, and the way in which the law can bring us into an intense experience of the power of sin—but it cannot do anything better than that. Now Paul describes the experience in fuller detail. *And sin taking opportunity through this command worked in me all covetousness.* He is viewing sin as a mighty power. This mighty magnetism towards wickedness actually makes use of your resolution not to sin. When the unconverted person seeks to stop coveting, and to control the desire for sin, sin gets a thousand times worse. When they use mere resolutions not to 'want' sin, and to 'want' only goodness and righteousness and holiness, unconverted people, people without Jesus, discover their appetite for sin is greater than they ever imagined. The more they try to be holy in this way the more they discover themselves to be a sewer of wickedness. And we shall just be burdened by the same experience if we seek to be godly in such a way.

Paul goes on to put this experience in two stages. Stage number one is: *For without the law sin is dead* (verse 8). *And I was alive without the law once . . .*

In stage number one of his experience he was 'without the law'. This does not mean that he knew nothing of the law. Every Jewish child knew the Mosaic law. But he had not seen the significance of the tenth command. The law was around but so far as the tenth command was concerned he was 'without the law'.

In stage number one of his experience, sin was dormant. He was not having a great struggle with sin and he felt all was well with his relationship to God. He was not aware of what a power sin is.

In stage number one of his experience, he was 'alive'. It means he was 'alive and well', he was at ease in life.

One day, something happened in Paul's life (or in the person into whose shoes he is putting himself). Stage number two of his experience is: *but when the command came, sin came to life* (verse 9) *and I died* (verse 10a).

In stage number two of his experience, he became conscious of the Tenth Commandment. The command 'came' to him. He started trying to keep it. Now 'the law' is painfully present—not in the 1500 or so bits of legislation which were a heavy burden but did not really affect the heart very much—they were not a problem. The burden upon him was not the 1500 commands, so much as the one: 'You shall not want . . . '

In stage number two of his experience, sin came to life! He had thought that sin was not much of a problem. He was a good Jew! He lived a good life, so he thought. But now he starts trying not to sin or even to want to sin, and he discovers powerful appetites within himself. All manner of wanting things he ought not to want are discovered within himself. He is so proud. He has such an appetite for glory. He is so insecure. He has such an appetite for money and possessions. His sexuality he thought was under control, but now he finds perhaps that it is a great problem that troubles him day and night. The law has awakened 'every kind of covetousness' (7:8).

In stage number two of his experience, Paul says, 'I died.' It means he fell into total helplessness. He is relating experience, and still expounding verse 5. He has already told us, 'when we were in the flesh, the sinful passions aroused by the law were at work in our bodies, so that we bore fruit for death.' Now he is putting the same point again, describing the experience. 'I died.' I produced fruit unto death. I was laden with guilt. I was further away from God than ever. I found no love for God in my heart. With all of my attempts to live a godly life the end product was death, Godlessness.

What is Paul's point in saying all of this? He is doing several things. Firstly, he is answering the question 'Is the law sin?' The answer is no, the law is not sinful. On the contrary the law powerfully sets itself against even the very desire for sin.

On the other hand Paul has another reason for saying all of this. Although the law is not sin, and is set against sin, it is entirely useless my trying to sanctify myself by it. The very essence of conversion, for Paul and for all of us in one way or another, is to be delivered from this way of trying to be holy. This is what it is like to be 'in the flesh' (7:5). If we ever seek to live a godly life by the law, we are moving from the Spirit to the flesh (see Gal. 3:1–5).

Paul wants to persuade us to live by Jesus, to live by the Spirit, to live without condemnation. To live by the law is to lapse back into 'the flesh' and into the experience where 'all manner of sinful desires' are stronger than ever. No, we need Jesus; we need release from condemnation; we need to refuse being laden with guilt; we live not by the flesh or by the law (the same thing!) but by being married to Jesus!

43

A DISCOVERY
ABOUT THE LAW
(Romans 7:10–12)

In stage number two of his experience, Paul (speaking for the unconverted person) said he made a discovery. *And the command which was to be unto life was found to me to be unto death.* Some people take this line as though it were hypothetical, as if it meant that if we could keep the law we could earn eternal life. But this interpretation is still thinking of Aquinas's moral code. 'If we could get perfect spirituality we could earn eternal life.'

But it is better to think of the actual law of the thirteenth century BC. Many times the law promised life. However, it was not eternal life that was in view. Rather it was national prosperity. If men and women honoured their parents, for example, it was promised that they would 'live', not live with eternal life, but 'live long in the land'. So the law promised life and the promise was quite genuine and sincere. There was nothing hypothetical about it.

But it is one thing for the law to promise national prosperity. It is another thing for anyone to think that he can get true spiritual life by an obedience that takes seriously the Tenth Commandment. Paul felt the law promised life. So it did! It promised life even if kept only partially (without reference to the Tenth Commandment). Even if it is kept externally by the citizens of a country it will do a certain amount of good. A country which does not lie or steal or where there is no adultery would 'live'. It would be a land of prosperity and stability. But it is entirely another thing for an individual standing before God to think he can keep the Tenth Commandment. It was at this point that Paul 'died'; he lost all hope.

He describes it further, *For sin, taking an opportunity through the law, deceived me and through the law killed me.* Here again Paul regards sin as a mighty power. Once again, he says sin used the law. It is not that the law is sinful. But sin is such a mighty power it can use even the holy and good law of God that God gave Israel for holy and good purposes. Sin took hold even of something that had a good purpose, and used it to kill people who misuse it, as did this person into whose position Paul is putting himself.

Sin deceives. It makes us feel that we can control our lives by law-keeping. But actually no matter how many times we assure ourselves we shall live a godly life, sin always defeats us when we seek to resist it by means of law-keeping, even to the extent of not coveting any kind of sin.

Paul comes to a conclusion in verse 12. *So then, on the one hand, the law is holy and the command is holy and righteous and good.*

It is 'holy' and 'sacred'. It had a special purpose; it was set aside by God for special use. It restrained sin in Israel. It separated Israel from the nations at the time when Israel needed to be separated from the nations. It is sacred in nature and in content.

It is righteous. It was taking steps to lead the people of God in the direction of holiness. It did not do this perfectly. It was designed for the hardness of heart of the people at the time. It allowed things that the teaching of Jesus did not allow. Yet taken on its own terms it was leading the people of God in the direction of righteousness.

The law is good. There is no place in the Bible where the law is said to come from any source other than God Himself. Negative language concerning the law is appropriate when considering the matter from the viewpoint of the New Covenant and the person-to-person relationship that the Christian has with God. The law is not for the righteous man; it does not control the Christian's person-to-person relationship with God. It does not justify (cf. Rom. 3:20); it does not sanctify or enable any kind of fruitfulness (cf. Rom. 7:4); it does not regenerate or give life (cf. Gal. 3:21). Yet taken upon its own terms and in its particular location in the history of salvation, it is entirely good, entirely beneficial, and is in no way *against* the promises of God (cf. Gal. 3:21). Its weakness arises from sinful man (cf. 'through the flesh', Rom. 8:3) not from its own inherent evil.

The precepts of God are altogether good in their intention and purpose. Despite the impression of inadequacy which one may glean from the Old Testament and which has been highlighted in previous sections, the law is never portrayed in any terms other than good ones. It is *inherently* good; it is altogether beneficient in its purpose.

The law is *God's* law. Although it is 'Mosaic' (and I use that phrase rather frequently as a protest against generalising concepts of the 'moral law'), yet within the Pentateuch its divine origin is emphasised.

It is 'good' for what it is designed to do. Although the New Testament criticises its use in certain respects, it may be 'used lawfully'. It was good for that which it was designed to do.

It must be remembered however that when one describes the law as 'holy, righteous and good', it is the whole law which is good, but it is so especially because of the Tenth Commandment, which looked into the heart of men and women and sets itself against their sin. It failed, but it was not the fault of the law that it failed; it was the fault of sin. The law is holy, righteous and good.

44

A SURVEY
(ROMANS 7:13–25)

We come now to get into the more controversial section of Romans, which is generally thought to be 7:14–25 (although actually the section begins in verse 13).

There is a wide range of opinions as to how the 'wretched man' of Romans should be taken. Let me make some comments and survey some interpretations at the same time.

(1) I start by saying that *corporate interpretations of the 'I' are not convincing*. Romans 7 is undoubtedly a profound chapter. It requires spiritual discernment to follow it. But it is *spiritual* discernment that is needed, not sheer cleverness. The letters of Paul are profound but they were written to ordinary people. I personally find it difficult to think that Paul wants his readers to guess (for there is no other way of knowing) that 'I' somehow means the entire nation of Israel or some kind of corporate 'Mr Everyman'. When 'I' means Israel, as perhaps it sometimes does in the Old Testament, the context makes it clear. It is not clear here. So I reject seeing the 'I' as Israel or as 'everyone' or as any kind of 'corporate' I. Similarly *I do not think the 'I' is Adam*. The command of Genesis 2 is not 'the law'. Adam was without the Mosaic law (see Rom. 5:14 compared with 20). The law never came to him. *Some interpretations are too far removed from the first-century style of thinking to be accepted as true interpretations of Paul.* I certainly doubt if the ordinary Christians at Rome could glean anything highly philosophical from Paul's letter to them.

I take it then that some kind of autobiographical interpretation is correct. The natural way to take the 'I' is that some individual is being described, maybe hypothetical, maybe some stage of a person's life.

(2) It is quite impossible that Paul should be referring to the 'normal' Christian. The 'norm' of the Christian life is not to say 'I am carnal'. The Christian says the exact opposite, in the sense of being dominated by sin. The normal Christian is not

ignorant of what he is doing (7:15), is not beset by failure (7:19–21), is not a prisoner (7:23), a slave (7:25b). This is the exact opposite of everything Paul has said in chapter 6. Above all the Christian can never, never, ask, 'Who shall deliver me?' He knows who the deliverer is!

(3) But I also assert that *it is quite impossible that the normal pagan can be referred to here*. This equally impossible. The man of Romans 7:13–25 and even in the whole of 7:7–25 is an extraordinarily 'spiritual' person! He has 'known' sin (7:7) and has had a battle with it. He does not *want* to sin. This in itself puts him apart from the average person, the 'person in the street'. The average, ordinary person does not care very much about sin. This person sees the spirituality of the Tenth Commandment. He knows that it judges his heart as well as his actions. He sees and understands there is such a thing as powerful 'desire' (7:8), pulling us into sin despite the commands not to even want to desire sin. He understands what it is for sin to be dormant (7:8) and for sin to 'come alive' with raging power (7:9). He knows his Old Testament and that the commandment was 'ordained to life'. He sees himself as a slave (7:14). (The normal unconverted person *is* a slave but he does not see himself that way). The man of 7:13–25 is a person who sees himself as a slave but has not found a way of deliverance. He has a great desire to be a holy person. What I mean is that there are good things he wants to do and there are sins he wants to avoid. He has a hatred of sin (7:15), although it does not say he has a love of righteousness!

(4) What other possibilities are there? If this person at the end of Romans chapter 7 really is an individual, yet he is neither a normal Christian nor a normal non-Christian, what other possibilities remain?

Is he a person before he has received sanctification? Is he a person being convicted by the law but not having found salvation? Is he the ill-taught Christian? I will give my answer and then argue it out later. *The wretched man of Romans 7:7 running right through to Romans 7:25 is a description of the maximum the holy law of God can do in the unconverted person.*

The law can show us how sinful we are. It can increase sinful desires and condemn us for the very fact that our desire for sin has increased. It can produce the conviction that we are a mass of sin. It can do all these things but it will always leave the unconverted person asking, 'Who can deliver me?'

45

GUIDELINES
(ROMANS 7:13–25)

I will not be able to give the 'last word' on Romans 7:13–25. But I would like to give at least some clear words and put the case for the interpretation I believe to be right.

(1) First of all, *the structure of the two final paragraphs of Romans 7 is clear and should be noted.*

Verse 7a	Question: Is the law sin?
Verse 7b	Answer: May it not be!
Verse 7c	Counter-proposal
Verse 7d–11	Development
Verse 12	Conclusion

Then once again:

Verse 13a	Question: Is the law sin?
Verse 13b	Answer: May it not be!
Verse 13c	Counter-proposal
Verse 14–25a	Development
Verse 25b	Conclusion

It is important to see that verses 7–12 and 13–25 go over the same ground twice. Paul did the same thing in chapter 6. Romans 6:1 asked a question and gave the answer, 'May it not be!' Romans 6:15 again asks a similar question and gives the same answer, which runs to 6:23. Then after some more exposition (7:1–6), 7:7 asks a question, gives an answer and develops it till 7:12. Then 7:13 asks yet a fourth question and for the fourth time gives the same answer: 'May it not be!'

Actually Paul's structure as one looks at 6:1–14, 6:15–23, 7:1–6, 7:7–12, 7:13–25 is a style of writing often found in the Bible (it is called a chiasmus), where material is presented in an A-B-C-B-A structure.

A. Can we sin? No! (6:1–14)
B. Can we sin? No! (6:15–23)
    C. *We died to the law (7:1–6)*
B. Is the law sin? No! (7:7–12)
A. Is the law sin? No! (7:13–25)

For me this is decisive proof that Romans 7:13–25 is a distinct sub-section, and verse 13 is certainly the beginning of the paragraph. This means that the change of tense in verse 14 is not very significant. It is mistaken to say that verse 14 begins a new section distinguished from the previous one by the present tense. Some have thought that verses 7–13 deal with the pre-Christian life and the shift in tense shows that verses 14–25 deal with the present Christian life. The truth is, verses 7–12 use a mixture of continuous past ('imperfect') and simple past ('aorist') tenses. And 7:13–25 is the extent of the paragraph; it begins with past tenses and switches into the present tense in verse 14, but the present tenses of verses 14–25 do not prove anything. Actually the section begins at 7:13 and has a past tense in it. And the switch to the present tense in verse 14 is only a vivid way of speaking, and nothing more. It certainly does not prove Paul is referring to his experience as a Christian.

(2) Secondly, *the development of the whole chapter should be noted and especially the place of verse 5.* He tells us we have died to the law (Romans 7:1–4) and then gives us a before-and-after comparison. Verse 5 deals with pre-conversion experience; verse 6 begins 'But now' and goes on to deal with what the Christian contrast is. We have died to the law in order to be fruitful towards God.

Romans 7:5–6 is the key. He compares what it is like to be 'in the flesh' and 'under the law' (on the one side) with being 'in the Spirit' (on the other side). But the vital point is, *verse 5 is a foreshadowing of verse 7–25.* Verse 5 talks about 'the flesh'; similarly Romans 7:14 takes up the matter of being 'of the flesh' and says 'nothing good dwells . . . in my flesh'. Verse 5 talks about sinful passions; similarly Romans 7:7–25 gives us a description of sinful passions. Verse 5 says the problem is aroused by the law; similarly Romans 7:7–25 is a detailed description of sin being aroused by the law. Verse 5 talks about sin at work in the bodily parts; similarly Romans 7:7–25 takes up this very matter (7:23, 24, 25b). Verse 5 talks about the end product, death. Romans 7:7–25 talks about the very same thing

(7:10, 11, 13, 24). *Everything in verse 5 is described in fuller detail in verses 7–25.* What is significant about this is that because verse 5 has a 'before and after' contrast, and 'in the flesh' clearly refers to the pre-salvation phase of life, then *this is proof positive that Romans 7:7–25 refers to the unregenerate phase of life.* This does not answer all questions, but it is a decisive matter. The same themes are there in verse 5 and in verses 7–25. The result of being under law (verse 5) is agony and spiritual death.

Romans 7 is in some sense being autobiographical. It is either actual autobiography or hypothetical autobiography. His using the present tense and his repeated 'if . . . if . . . ' suggests that it is describing one person's personal experience, but that Paul was not currently experiencing what he describes. The sheer misery of verse 24 was surely not Paul's there and then experience. This makes us think that it is a hypothetical description of what it is like when 'I' go through a certain situation. He is either describing himself at some stage of his life, or he is using a preacher's 'I' where a preacher puts himself in the position of a certain individual and says, 'If I do this, and if I do that . . . ' and goes on to use 'I' but is putting himself in the position of some case that he is thinking of.

(3) The dominant theme of the chapter is freedom from the law. It is this—I believe—that gives us the answer. Paul has been telling us that we are free from the law, and contrasting what it is like to be under the law. *The wretched man of Romans 7:7 running right through to Romans 7:25 is a description of the maximum the holy law of God can do in the unconverted person.*

46

BONDAGE TO SIN
(ROMANS 7:13–15)

Romans 7:13 starts a new paragraph. It is a question similar to verse 7 but not exactly the same. *Then did this good thing become death to me?* It is a question similar to verse 7 but that verse asks whether the law is evil in itself ('Is the law sin?'). Now verse 13 asks a slightly different question. Admitting that the law is not evil in itself, is it on the side of sin and death? Is it a case of a good thing being used for evil? Is the law itself a conveyer of death? The answer is still no. *Let it not be!*

Paul explains God's purpose in this. The law was not sinful. *On the contrary, it was sin working death to me through what is good, in order that sin might be shown to be sin, and this was in order that sin might become exceedingly sinful through the commandment* (Rom. 7:13). This is the crucial statement of the paragraph. It was not the law that brought death to the unconverted Paul. It was sin that killed him. It brought such covetousness, such increased wickedness, such guilt and shame that any relationship with God was impossible. The agony of defeat and intensified shame that some unconverted people go through is allowed by God. What is His purpose in it? Not everyone goes through this agony before they are saved, but some do. They start trying to live a godly life, they seek to be holy, they try to measure up to God's holy law. It leads to the kind of intense agony that Paul is about to describe. Why does God allow it at all? It is one way of discovering the exceeding sinfulness of sin. (There are other ways. Job made the same discovery through suffering.) Our unregenerate hearts are vile, ugly, deceitful above all things, desperately wicked. But the Tenth Commandment was one way God had of teaching the man or woman who sought salvation and holiness 'in the flesh' how wicked he or she was. This is Paul's point. Let the unconverted person try it! Let the unconverted person try 'in the flesh' to cease coveting and to cease as a result of coveting from falling into all sorts of sin. What he will discover is the truth of Romans 7:5. The law will inflame sin. The terrible bondage he falls into only shows how powerful sin is. Through the commandment, the Tenth Commandment in particular, sin will become more powerful than ever! It will gain power. He will get to see how strong the sinful nature is. This is the point of Romans 7:13–25. It is repeating verses 7–12 but going into the matter more thoroughly and it is again a development of Romans 7:5.

Verse 14 begins to explain and expound. *For I know (on the one hand) that the law is spiritual, but I myself (on the other hand) am carnal, sold into bondage by sin.* The Greek can be translated as 'we know' (*oidamen*) or as 'I know, on the one hand' (*oida men*). The letters of the original Greek were run together and the divisions (*oidamen* or *oida men*) is a matter of interpretation. Since Paul says 'me . . . me' in verse 13 and continues 'I . . . I' through the rest of the paragraph, it is likely that 'I' is to be found here. This is especially true if the paragraph begins in verse 13.

The person who discovers the great power and evil of sin is one who seeks to keep the law knowing its spirituality. Paul still has the Tenth Commandment in mind. The law is spiritual. It was given by the Holy Spirit and by means of the Tenth Commandment it can search into the hearts of men and women. People who come under the law in this way, however, discover that they are carnal. The word means 'dominated by the flesh'. It is precisely this that Paul denies is true of the Christian in Romans 8:5–9. The Christian is not 'carnal' or 'fleshly' in the sense of being *ruled* by the flesh. Paul repeats the thought of verse 5, 'when we were in the flesh'. (In 1 Corinthians 3:1–5 there is a different use of the word where it means immature, living in an inconsistent way. That is not relevant here. The person of Romans 7:13–25 is not carnal in *that* sense; he delights in God's Mosaic law.) Certainly the word 'carnal' rules out the possibility that this person is a 'normal' Christian.

This person under the law is also 'sold into bondage under sin'. He is utterly and totally a slave (and therefore this is not the normal Christian). Yet he sees himself as a slave and freely confesses himself to be a slave (and therefore is not the normal unconverted person who does not view himself in that way). It is neither the normal Christian nor the normal non-Christian. It is rather the unconverted person unusually and powerfully under the law. It is not describing a part of the person or an aspect of his life. Paul is dealing with what the man is as a whole.

This carnality is seen in this person's struggles and his bewildered defeat. It is bewildering for him. He says *For I do not understand what I am doing.* And it is defeat. *For the thing that I do is not what I want to do, but what I am hating is the very thing I do (Rom. 7:15).* This is radical and serious failure. Still it is not describing a part of the person or an aspect of his life. Paul is dealing with what the man as a whole is experiencing. It is not an occasional matter, but the life viewed as a whole.

This is a description of the person who sees the spirituality of the law and desires to keep it, yet is unconverted. What can the law of God do for him? It only brings him to see the exceedingly sinfulness of sin (7:13), because he is carnal (7:14), a slave (7:14), as is seen in his general defeat (7:15).

47

LIVING WITH FAILURE
(Romans 7:16–18)

We are looking at the unconverted man, 'under the law'. We need to try to keep the whole thread of Paul's argument before us.

Verse 13 lays down the basic statement. God allows men and women to come under the law in order to show them the great power of sin.

Verse 14 begins to explain how this works out in practice. Such a person discovers himself to be carnal, and a slave to sin. Verse 15 tells us of the way in which such a person is regularly and frequently defeated as he seeks to keep the tenth commandment.

Now in verses 16 and 17 we have two deductions from all of this. The first deduction is this: *And if I do the very thing that I do not wish to do, I am agreeing that the law is good* (Rom. 7:16). In the experience of conviction of sin I am not regarding the Tenth Commandment as an evil thing. Paul is still answering the questions of verses 7 and 13. Is the law something evil or which functions in an evil way? No, it is entirely good, but it is used by God to demonstrate that I am thoroughly evil and wicked!

Then comes Paul's second deduction. *But now it is no longer I that am working this thing but rather it is sin which is living inside me* (Rom. 7:17). This is an amazing statement. Here is an unregenerate person. He is not the *normal* unregenerate person (who definitely does not have the kind of spiritual insight we see here!). But on the other hand he is definitely not the normal regenerate person either, who certainly cannot describe himself as a slave and defeated, and so on. Here is a description of the very *best* the law could possibly do. The best it could possibly do is to produce a duality between 'I' and 'I'. Here is a person with a divided being. It is not 'me' doing this thing (if the bad English may be forgiven!), yet sin is dwelling in 'me'. It *is* me but it is *not* me. I *don't* want to do it but I *do* do it. This is the best that the law can do. It can produce a state in me where I deny and disown what I am doing—and yet I do it! Immense guilt is the result. I feel awful. I just know that what I am doing is wrong and there is something in me that does not want to do this thing, and yet so great is the power of covetousness within me, that I cannot stop myself. I fall every time! This is the very best state that an unconverted person can get to, as he struggles to be spiritual by keeping the Mosaic law in the form of the Tenth Commandment.

Verses 18 to 20 explain this last point in verse 17 more fully. *For I know that there does not dwell in me, that is in my flesh, any good thing. For the willing to do the good thing is present in me, but to carry it out is not!* (Rom. 7:18). He is explaining more of this duality. Keep in mind, we are dealing with the unconverted person who—although he is unconverted—is intensely seeking to carry out the law, especially the Tenth Commandment. The law is powerfully calling upon him to live a godly life internally and spiritually. He must not even desire something that would be in the slightest degree sinful for him. He, in his self-righteousness, wants to obey this law. Yet his personality is dominated by 'the flesh', the sinful side of our personality. In the unconverted person it rules and reigns over him. Notice the contrast between this passage (about the unconverted person) and Romans 8:5–9. The Christian is not in the flesh. The unconverted person *is* in the flesh and he is ruled over by it. Most would not care about the Tenth Commandment. But if anyone ever does seek to obey it—for whatever reason—he will find that 'the flesh' is too strong for him. He is 'in Adam'. All his resolutions fail. The Christian person is capable of mortifying the flesh (Rom. 6:12; 8:12–13), but to live under the law does not mortify the flesh. Rather it fortifies the flesh. It invigorates the 'flesh' and makes it more powerful than ever.

We must notice too the difference between Romans chapter 6 and Romans 7:7–25. In Romans 6 'I' have died to sin, 'I' am risen with Christ. My essential personality is in Christ and I am able to resist the 'flesh' (that side of my nature which is able to feel the pull of sin). But here in Romans 7 'I' is identified with 'flesh'. The Paul of Romans 6 would not have said 'me, that is my flesh'. This unconverted person is not *correcting* himself; he is rather identifying himself with flesh.

This is why the Christian must grasp hold of what Paul has said in Romans 7:4 and 6. The Christian has died to the law through the fact that Jesus died for him in His body on the cross. He is now not married to the law; he is married to Jesus. He should never directly look at the law at all. Let the Christian look to the heavenly husband, Jesus. Looking to Jesus will bring forth fruit unto God. Rejoicing in salvation will bring forth fruit unto God. Persistent faith in the promises of God, responsiveness to the Holy Spirit.

There can never be fruitful living unless there is the joy of the Lord, and the Mosaic law can never produce the joy of the Lord.

Paul is wanting to persuade these Christians in Rome to base their lives on what he has said to them in Romans 5 and 6. They are free from the law. This is the best that the law can do in an unconverted person. Let them not try to live on the law; that would be going back to 'the flesh' in the most extreme way. They have begun in the Spirit (the one matter that is not mentioned in Romans 7:7–25!). Let them not turn from the Spirit to the law. This is the best the law could ever do for anyone! It can induce despair but it can do nothing more. Let them live in Jesus and in the power of the Spirit.

48

PARTIAL CONVICTION
(Romans 7:19–23)

The best thing the law can do is to produce a 'spiritually-minded' person who is a total failure! There is enough of the general working of the Spirit and of conscience in every person for that person to know about sin and evil. When the law of God and the Tenth Commandment is added into the situation it can produce a certain kind of unconverted 'spirituality'. But what it cannot do is bring about victory over sin or freedom of conscience. It does not open our eyes to Jesus. It does not even *really* convict of sin because the person concerned has got the idea that he or she can fulfil the law. He knows he never does keep the law but he is always trying. He says—I know that the will to do good is present with me, but to carry it out is not, but I will have one more try. This time I really *will* carry it out—and then he fails again. He is not *really* convinced of his inability and sinfulness. Such a person is only *partially* 'convicted' of his sinfulness. It takes the Holy Spirit to really convict of sin. The Bible never says the law convicts of sin; it says the Spirit convicts of sin. The law convicts of sin *partially*.

In Romans 7:18–20 Paul is explaining this divided mentality that he first mentioned in verse 17. He continues, *For I do not do the good thing I want to do, but instead the bad thing I do not want to do is the very thing I do* (Rom. 7:19). Verse 19 more or less repeats verse 15. This person is a permanent failure despite all of his desires. There is a clash between wanting and doing. 'I do not do the good thing I want . . . '. There is a contradiction between theory and practice.

Verse 20 repeats the thought of 17. *And if what I do not want is the very thing I do, it is no longer that I am working this thing but it is this sin dwelling in me.* Here again he mentions this state where I deny and disown what I am doing—and yet I do it! The power of sin overrides all my good intentions. Here again is the very best state that an unconverted person can get to, as he struggles to be spiritual by keeping the Tenth Commandment.

The words 'no longer' are important. It shows that something has happened to this person. He is 'no longer' what he was. It does not mean that Paul is referring to the regenerate person. But it does show he is 'no longer' the normal unconverted person. The law has come to him. He is trying to live the Tenth Commandment. He is 'no longer' living the kind of complacent life that some people live. but he has not discovered Jesus either! He is not even mentioning Jesus' name. He is not saved. He is unsaved. but he is 'no longer' the casual worldling he used to be. We follow the argument and remember that verse 13 lays down the basic statement; God allows people to come under the law to show them the great power of sin. Verses 14, 15 explain further. Such a person is carnal (14), a slave (14) and is generally defeated (15). Verses 16–17 draw some deductions. The law is good (16); sin is the problem (17). Verses 18 to 20 explain this last point in verse 17 more fully. Indwelling sin is the problem of man.

Now verse 21 lays down another statement and goes a step further. *So then*—he is summarising where he has got to in his argument—*I find this law belongs to me, although I want to do the good thing, that the evil thing is close by me.* He says there is another kind of law, another kind of powerful governing principle. The powerful operating of sin in my life is actually more powerful than the law of God, and the law of God is insufficient to overthrow it. Paul is restating what he said in verses 14 and 15. He is carnal, he is a slave, he is defeated. Now he puts it another way. There is a power rule operating in his life, more powerful than the law of God. He explains what he means. *For I happily agree with the law of God in the inner man . . .* (Rom. 7:22). This man seems quite spiritual at this point. Some have thought he is regenerate because he happily agrees with the law of God. But actually it is no mark of godliness to be trying to get to be a godly person by the law. We are meant to happily agree with the law, but we are not meant to delude ourselves that happily agreeing with the law will help us in the least. It will not. And the unconverted man can happily agree with the law. Pharisees love it.

The phrase 'inner man' must not be overused. Verses 23 and 25 show that it does mean anything more than 'mind'. This person intellectually reckons he can be a godly person. But the law is only in his mind. It is not in his life and actual conduct.

'Happily agreeing' with the law is not quite the same as what the psalmists say when they delight in the law day and night. The Hebrew word for *law* is a very much wider word and means teaching rather than 'legislation'. It is one thing to delight day and night in the teaching of God. It is another thing to delight in Mosaic legislation with the Tenth Commandment as its sharpest point. Paul especially has the Tenth Commandment in mind. Psalm 1 had a much wider reference.

The trouble is, despite this person's happily agreeing with the law of God, he has to say, *but I see another law in my members at war with the law of my mind and taking me captive with the law of sin which is in my members* (Rom. 7:23). This person who happily agrees with the law of God, especially with the Tenth Commandment and its powerful and internal forbidding of sin, is nevertheless enslaved. He is totally incapable of throwing off the powerful domineering 'law'. He needs to be in an entirely different position before he will be able to live a godly life.

49

DEFEATED GODLINESS
(Romans 7:24–25)

We have seen some of the characteristics of this person who is trying to get to be holy by living under the law of Moses. He experiences the power of sin (7:7). All manner of sinful desires are let loose as he struggles not to want sin (7:8). He 'dies', that is, he is reduced to total hopelessness (7:9–11, 13). He comes into bewildered defeat (7:15–16), and a divided mind (7:17–20). The end of verse 23 puts a picture of him as entirely and securely taken prisoner by the power of sin. The person under the law has a powerful dictator, sin, within himself, who has him utterly and totally within his grasp (7:21–23).

Verse 24 follows. *Miserable person that I am! Who shall deliver me out of the body of this death?*

He is unhappy; he cries out, 'Miserable person that I am!' He is ignorant and in despair; he asks *who* can deliver him. He is conscious of his bondage; he asks for deliverance. Yet he has enough spiritual perception to know of his plight, to know he needs a deliverer, and to know that the problem is indwelling sin in his body. This is all that the law can do.

The question might be asked, 'Can a Christian go through any of this?' I answer as follows. The Christian may know something of it but he never uses the word 'Who?', and he knows the answer to his plight whereas this person does not! The Christian can find himself temporarily looking to some kind of law. When he does that he will have an experience similar to the one at the end of Romans 7 but he will never come to the cry of despair. He will never say, 'Who . . . ?' He knows who! Jesus.

And this means that when he does have a taste of such an experience he should know what to do about it. He turns away from the law and he turns back speedily to Jesus!

At this point it is as though Paul can bear the strain and the gloom of this chapter no more. He interrupts with an inserted burst of praise. *(Thanks be to God through our Lord Jesus*

Christ!)   It certainly is an interruption. Paul is not saying
'Thanks be to God that I am miserable!' And he is not saying
'Thanks be to God that I serve the law of God with my mind but
with my flesh serve the law of sin.' Paul's remark does not
connect either with what precedes or with what follows. It is an
interruption.

Then he comes to a final conclusion and summary. *So
then I myself on the one hand serve the law of God with the mind, but
with the flesh I serve the law of sin.*

This is how sin works when someone is seeking holiness
by the law. The mind and the flesh contradict each other. We
have all made promises to ourselves about godly living but then
the flesh has defeated us. Paul's concluding words are a
summary of defeated godliness. *So then . . .* , says Paul, ending
his paragraph with a summary and a conclusion, *I myself (on the
one hand) serve the law of God with the mind, but in the flesh I serve
the law of sin.*

Again we have to say he is describing what it is like when
a sincere person tries with religious sincerity to live a godly life
by focusing on the law of Moses. In Romans 7:5 and from
Romans 7:7 onwards he has been referring to people doing so 'in
the flesh' (that is, as unconverted people), but his message is
relevant to the Christian as well. For a Christian to go back to the
Mosaic law is the same mistake as for him to go back to sin. To
turn to law-keeping is backsliding, as much moral sin. Both are
turning away from the gospel. Both will bring forth fruit unto
death.

It is easy to *think* we can have victory over sin by keeping
the law. When someone is just *thinking* about it all is well. 'I
myself serve the law of God with the mind.' He is able to
imagine himself having victory in such a way. He imagines
himself keeping the law of God. He thinks how wonderful
God's law is. He actually deludes himself that he will keep it.

But then an actual situation of pressure to sin comes
along. When that happens the mind is of no value at all. All the
wonderful fantasising about obedience suddenly deserts us.
Something that is much more powerful than the mind (in the
person who is seeking to live by the law) takes over, the power of
the flesh! Remember chapter 6 where Paul spoke of the power of
the 'body of sin' (6:6) and the slavery set up by sin (6:6–16, 17).
Remember 7:5 and its talk about the power of the flesh.

In the person trying to live by law—even God's law given

to Israel—the conflict between theory and practice, between mind and flesh, is overwhelming. It is the Spirit that leads us to 'fulfil' the law (8:1–4), but not by being 'under' the law! If we walk in the Spirit deliberately, we shall 'fulfil' the law accidentally!

Paul has simply been telling us of the best that the law can do. If we focus on the commandment not to covet it can bring even the unconverted, undelivered person to a high appreciation of spirituality. But the law cannot actually work that spirituality in him The bottom line is in Romans 7:25b. It leads us to holiness in theory, but defeat in practice. Such a person serves God in the mind and imagination, but out in the real world falls again and again to the power of the flesh.

What then is the answer? The law does not have it. Anyone who tries to get to be a holy person by focusing on the law of God is doomed to end up with Romans 7:25b, a conflict between mind and flesh, with the flesh as the decided winner! Are you trying to live this way? Are you really succeeding? I do not think so.

50

LIVING FOR GOD
(Romans 7:25a)

When Paul gave his interrupting burst of praise to God, it was because he in himself knew something entirely different from all this agony he had been describing.

What in fact was he rejoicing at? He was thanking God for knowing his release from the law of God. The law is no more help to us than the flesh! It is a surprising thing that the law should be bracketed with sin. We have to die to that horrid thing called sin. But—amazingly—we even have to die in precisely the same way to the holy and righteous and good law of God. The law will not help us any more than sin could help us. We shall bring forth fruit unto death if we live under sin. We shall bring forth fruit unto death if we live under the holy law of God. Of course we do not die to holiness, but we die to a particular way of trying to get to that holy life. To walk in the Spirit actually fulfils and more-than-fulfils the law of Israel. Jesus' level of spirituality is higher than the Mosaic law.

Godly living comes not by a relationship with Jesus that runs via the law, but a relationship with Jesus that is direct. Sanctification comes by faith in Jesus plus faith in Jesus plus more faith in Jesus. Godliness consists of the works of faith not the works of the law. Try it! It works!

It is fellowship with Jesus that is the secret of holy living. Holiness is living for God. It is love for people, and more love, and more love. It is being like Jesus.

God accepts us in Jesus even before there is much practical holiness in our lives. We are 'sanctified' in Jesus for ever, before we are actually sanctified in ourselves. Holiness comes to us indirectly. It is true that we can have very direct leadings of the Holy Spirit, but the real power for godliness comes indirectly. It comes when we are rejoicing, when we see that we have died to sin and are risen in Christ.

See the distinction between our self and our bodies

(Romans 6). Sin is not in us; it is only in our bodies. This gives us a great sense of triumph over sin. Know that your new self is not in the kingdom of sin at all and is risen with Christ.

Seek outpourings of the Holy Spirit. Impetus is given to the life of godliness when we have 'rivers of living water'. Follow the leading of the Spirit. Be much in fellowship with Jesus, feeding on Him as the bread of life. Jesus is to be our daily food. We are in a living personal relationship to Him. Cease trying to be holy by law-keeping and start relating to Jesus directly. Holiness comes by living on Jesus directly, not by a holiness mediated through the law. Holiness is without the law—although indirectly it does 'fulfil the law'. Forget about the law of God for the moment. Realise that Jesus is your Saviour. Realise that you are holy in Him. See that He has taken you out of the kingdom of sin altogether. Then start resisting sin.

The Holy Spirit will make plain to you what are the works of the flesh. You will not need any special guidance in the matter. 'The works of the flesh are plain!' You do not need the law of God to know that to worship some pagan god is sin (the First Commandment), or that to worship God under the form of some painting or statue is sin (the Second Commandment), or that to use the name of God to your own advantage is sin (the Third Commandment). You will know those things without having to consult the Ten Commandments. Yes, of course the Ten Commandments describe them as sin, but did you have to look them up to know? The works of the flesh are plain to everyone who has been born again by the Spirit of God. You know that you ought to respect parents (the Fifth Commandment). You would feel bad if you killed anyone (the Sixth Commandment) or if you committed adultery (the Seventh Commandment) or stole (the Eighth Commandment) or lied (the Ninth Commandment). You do not need the external commandments to know these things are sin. The works of the flesh are obvious!

You give God the 'members' of your body and put them at His disposal to do whatever He leads you to. Make progress as Jesus speaks His Word to you by His Spirit. Speedily get to hear the voice of God by meditating on God's written Word. As you read the Mosaic legislation, do not put yourself under it. Ask: how is the Holy Spirit leading me to 'fulfil' this and outstrip it? When you read about murder, Jesus will talk to you about anger. When you read about adultery, Jesus will talk to you about purity. You will be going beyond the law. You will be careful not to put yourself under such a low standard as the Mosaic legislation. Keep in fellowship with Jesus and His cleansing blood. The one thing to focus on is love, seeing things from the other person's point of view (Matt. 7:12), being like Jesus to others, making others feel forgiven, wanted, valued, encouraged. Maintain your joy and keep yourself in the love of God. Cultivate skill in recognising temptation and cutting it off at its earliest stages. Expect God to give you extra help by chastening you! Accept His rebukes. Painful events are there to teach you. When things are going wrong they are going right! Let patience have its perfect work. Resist the devil. Attend to the detailed instructions of Jesus. Grow in wisdom. Grow in skill at working out how to live. Learn your weaknesses. When you fail, get up again. Receive the forgiveness of God. Go forward in prayer and more prayer and more prayer. Learn to give quantity time and quality time to God. Regard yourself as at best an unprofitable servant. If you ever say, 'I thank you that I am not as other people,' laugh at yourself for being such a fool! Belong to Jesus ' . . . who has been raised from the dead so that we may bear fruit for God.' Be happy slaves 'in the new life of the Spirit'. 'Who will deliver me?' Jesus already has!

OASIS BIBLE STUDY SERIES

The **Oasis Bible Study Series** has been designed to help Christians apply the Word of God to their lives and grow in their faith. Every book contains 31 undated studies, each of which provides teaching on a relevant theme and suggests ways in which that teaching may be applied to everyday life.

There are also exercises to help you work out in practice what you're learning on paper. The exercises will involve you in meditation and memorisation of Scripture, writing down your own opinions, and practical assignments.

The studies have been handled by different internationally renowned authors who have been specifically chosen because of their proven effectiveness in a particular area of teaching and ministry.

Available in this series:

Believing God	R. T. Kendall
The Church and You	Terry Virgo
The Church in the World	Charles Colson
Dynamic Intercession	Mike Bickle
For New Christians	Terry Virgo
God's Amazing Grace	Terry Virgo
God's Miraculous Power	Mahesh Chavda
The Gospel to the Poor	John Wimber
Personal Evangelism	Larry Tomczak
Spiritual Disciplines	C. J. Mahaney
Values for Living	Tony Campolo
Vision for the Nations	Kriengsak Chareonwongsak
Walk by the Spirit	Michael Eaton

Oasis Bible Notes series

WALK BY THE SPIRIT

MICHAEL EATON

If someone asked you, 'How do you walk by the Spirit?' what answer would you give? Michael Eaton takes you systematically through Galatians chapters 5 and 6 and provides clear teaching on the way that God wants you to live.

He points out that the Galatian Christians were losing the joy of their salvation because they were trying to put themselves under the Mosaic Law. Then he helps you to recognise and overcome legalism in your own life. He introduces the law of love and explains how you can resist temptation and develop the fruit of the Spirit.

Catalogue Number YB 9807 £1.99

Oasis Bible Notes series

GOD'S AMAZING GRACE

TERRY VIRGO

Many people are frustrated when they know the ideal but fail to reach it and 'reign in life'. With particular reference to the books of Romans and Galatians, the author builds a solid foundation of grace and reveals how 'reigning' is possible. Among the subjects he discusses are: our righteousness in Christ; legalism; personal discipline; condemnation; temptation; and freedom from sin.

Catalogue Number YB 9801   £1.99

Oasis Bible Notes series

BELIEVING GOD

R. T. KENDALL

Believing God—that's the definition of faith. When God tells us that He will do something, we believe Him and we wait with complete confidence that He will fulfil His promise.

'Faith accomplishes extraordinary things,' says R. T. Kendall, who underlines this claim by looking into the mighty exploits of those mentioned in Hebrews 11. He explains that our generation will face challenges for which there is no precedent, and encourages us to imitate the faith of those who stood firm when breakthrough seemed humanly impossible, because they trusted solely in the promises of God.

Catalogue Number YB 9805   £1.99

Oasis Bible Notes series

SPIRITUAL DISCIPLINES

C. J. MAHANEY

'I said to the Lord, "What's my problem with prayer?" And He replied, "You don't do it!" ' That was the stark reality that hit C. J. Mahaney before he got down to disciplining his Christian life. Now he passes on some of the things he's learned.

Jesus engaged in *Spiritual Disciplines*. There was a clear connection between His secret devotion and His public power. C. J. Mahaney challenges you to make the sacrifices necessary to 'perform at peak level' and makes practical suggestions about how you can develop self-control and avoid many seemingly innocent activities that hinder your service for God.

Catalogue Number YB 9802   £1.99